THE
Feuds of the Clans

BY THE

Rev. ALEXANDER MACGREGOR, M.A.

TOGETHER WITH

THE HISTORY

OF THE

FEUDS AND CONFLICTS

AMONG THE CLANS

IN THE NORTHERN PARTS OF SCOTLAND
AND IN THE WESTERN ISLES,

FROM THE YEAR MXXXI UNTO MDCXIX

First published in 1764 "from a MS. wrote in the reign of King James VI.

1907.

NOTE.

THE first part of this book was written by the late Rev. Alexander Macgregor, M.A., on 21st October, 1875, and delivered as a lecture to the Working Men's Club at Inverness on 19th November, 1875.

The second part is from a MS. written in the reign of King James VI., and first published in 1764 by Messrs. Foulis, Glasgow; reprinted by Messrs. Robertson, Glasgow, in 1780; and again reprinted in *Miscellanea Scotica*, Vols. I.-II., 1818. It was also reprinted in the *Celtic Magazine*, Vol. XI., 1885-1886.

CONTENTS.

	PAGE
THE FEUDS OF THE CLANS,	1
THE DESCRIPTION OF SUTHERLAND,	51
CONFLICTS—	
The Conflict of Drumilea,	53
The Conflict of Embo,	54
The Conflict of Bealach-na-Broige,	55
The Conflict of Clachnaharry,	56
The Conflict of Clan Chattan and Clan Kay,	58
The Conflict of Tuiteam-Tarbhach,	59
The Conflict of Lon-Harpasdal,	61
The Conflict of Druimnacoub,	61
The Conflict of Ruaig-Shansaid,	65
The Conflict of Blar-Tannie,	66
The Conflict of Blar-na-Pairc,	67
The Conflicts of Skibo and Strathfleet,	68
The Crowner Slain by the Keiths in the Chapel of St. Tayre,	69
The Conflict of Aldicharrish,	70
The Skirmish of Dail-Riabhach,	72
The Conflict of Torran Dubh,	73
The Conflict of Alltan-Beath,	75
The Conflict of Garbharry,	77

viii   Contents

CONFLICTS (*continued*)—   PAGE
    The Burning of the Dornoch Cathedral, ...   79
    The Conflicts of Allt-Gamhna and Leckmelm,   82
    Troubles in the Western Isles in the Year
        1586, ...   84
    The Troubles Between Sutherland and Caith-
        ness in 1587-90, ...   96
    The Troubles Between the Earls of Huntly
        and Moray, ...   101
    The Troubles Betwixt the Forbeses and the
        Gordons in the Years 1571 and 1572, ...   120
    The Brig of Dee, ...   129
    A Tumult in Ross in 1597, ...   131
    The Death of Sir Lauchlan Maclean in 1598,   132
    Troubles in the West Isles Betwixt the Clan
        Donald and the Siol Tormoit in 1601,...   136
    The Troubles Between Lord Kintail and
        Glengarry, ...   140
    Troubles in the Island of Raasay in 1611,... 141
    The Troubles of the Lewis, ...   145
    Some Troubles Betwixt Sutherland and
        Caithness in 1612, ...   156
    The Spanish Blanks, and What Follows
        Thereupon, ...   160

The Feuds of the Clans.

THE Highlands and Islands have in no previous age received greater attention, in regard to their natural beauties, than in these latter times. Until within the last thirty or forty years these romantic territories were almost a *terra incognita* to such tourists as now frequent them in hundreds, and were known only to the natives, and to such as, in piratical and feudal times, made bloody inroads upon them. Until of comparatively late years, those interesting localities were next thing to inaccessible to the southerns from the want of roads, and of all sorts of public conveyances. Indeed, of old, few tourists ever thought for a moment of crossing the Moray Frith, but still fewer were even aware of the splendid scenery that is to be found, towards the western coasts of Inverness, Ross, and Sutherland shires, and the many interesting isles that lie beyond. Even still, there are many lakes, mountains, and localities of interest that remain but very partially explored in Coigeach, Assynt, and the internal regions of the county of Sutherland. It is but of late that the singular natural embrasures of the beautiful Loch Maree have been seen. Until within the last few years the rough country pathway was quite impassable for wheeled carriages of every description, and even to the traveller, if a stranger, it was anything but pleasant. The consequence was that few indeed had ever seen it but the natives alone. Pennant and M'Culloch are, we believe, the only two scientific men who, until of late years, had visited it. But how rich the reward when attained! The mountains around the lake are of great height, and of a beautifully characterised and irregular outline. The shores present an immense variety of very interesting and romantic scenery. In fact, the mountains, and the loch, with its many islands, are among the finest specimens of the grand and picturesque to be found in Scotland.

The Isle of Skye, likewise, lay in the same secluded state as to its natural curiosities until within the last half-century. I remember, myself, when the now far-famed Quiraing was but little seen and still less known. The same may be said of Loch-cor-uisge, the Spar Cave, the Cullin Hills, and the other endless varieties of grand scenery in that distinguished isle. Sir Walter Scott with his pen, Horatio M'Culloch and others with their pencils, were among the first to bring Cor-uisge into notice. The Spar Cave, commonly called "Slochd Altraman," was at first discovered by the crew of a boat who took shelter from the storm in the mouth of the cave, who kindled a fire there, and by the light of it observed the lofty vaulted cave, sparkling with its pure white icicles of semi-transparent spar. But what a change has been effected by the lapse of a few years! These and hundreds of other localities in those interesting regions are now annually visited by hordes of eager tourists from every quarter of the kingdom, as well as from distant parts of the world. Very much credit for this mighty change is due to the Companies of the Highland, Sutherland, Caithness, and Skye Railways, which have opened up more of the Highlands and Islands in a few years than has ever been done before. By means of these enterprising Companies, cheap and easy access can now be had to every parish and province in the far north and west. The most distant corners of the land, from John o' Groat's to the Butt of Lewis, are brought within the range of a day's journey. Mountains and lakes, glens and dales, forests and plains, may be seen gliding past as if in a panoramic view when the inexhaustible iron horse speeds its rapid course along. Railways will create a revolution in the manners, customs, and language of the Highlands and Islands. Whilst our Gaelic Societies and our Celtic enthusiasts are straining their efforts to the utmost to prolong the existence and to preserve the speaking of the Gaelic tongue, the iron-horse alone is more powerful to counteract than are all their efforts to foster the progress of the Celtic language. The railway, although unintentionally, will do more to undermine the advancement of the Celtic as a spoken language in the Highlands than a battalion of Blackies around a Celtic chair, or delivering eloquent lectures in every Highland town and parish, can possibly achieve to cherish it. In one point of view this is to be regretted, but in another it is not. Every philanthropist must acknowledge that two different languages spoken in two sections of a kingdom cannot tend to the civilisation of those who speak not the language of the nation at large. The sooner the sections become amalgamated and assimilated to each other in customs and language the better. The Highlanders are now, and ever were, faithful and fearless, and it is surely very delightful to see such qualities still existing in all their pristine strength, and existing, too, without that alloy of fierceness and ferocity which characterised them in the turbulence of feudal times. The Highlanders had their faults, no doubt, but a peculiar political situation was the cause of their faults, and that which swept away the cause has rendered the effects a tale of olden times.

I have said that the railway has opened up the romantic recesses of Skye and the other isles to the delighted tourist, but another cause has operated powerfully to attract numberless sight-seers to the "Isle of Mist" to witness not only many points of attraction, but likewise other localities which, in olden times, were the scenes of many skirmishes and bloody feuds. That other cause is simply this—the eloquent, graphic, racy description of Skye given by my good friend, Sheriff Alexander Nicolson of Kirkcudbright, in his late articles contributed to "Good Words." Himself a son of the "Isle of Mist," gentle and generous, clannish and kind-hearted, to the back-bone a Highlander, the account given by him of his native isle is worthy of himself. The learned Sheriff has likewise published lately in a monthly periodical called the "Gael," a beautiful poetical description of Skye scenery, both in Gaelic and English, of which I may give a brief specimen in each of these languages. The learned gentleman says in Gaelic:—

  An toigh leat na beanntan mòr,
  Cruachan 's na neoil gu h-ard?
  Coireachan, frithean, dachaidh an fhìr-eoin,
   'San cluinnear na h-easan a' gàir'.

The Feuds of the Clans

An toil leat na glacagan grianach,
Innìsean sgiamhach na'm bò,
Iuàghan 'bheir fonn ri guth nan tonn?
Siubhail gu Innis a' cheò!

Translated—

Lovest thou mountains great,
  Peaks to the clouds that soar,
Corrie and fell, where eagles dwell,
  And cataracts dash evermore?

Lovest thou green grassy glades,
  By the sunshine sweetly kist,—
Murmuring waves and echoing caves?
  Then go to the "Isle of Mist."

Of Cor-uisge and Quiraing the Sheriff says:—

An Coruisg chi thu sud fo dhùbh-ghrùaim,
Cùl-uamhais measg strìth nan dùl;
'Nuair bhriseas an torunn le fuaim na doininn,
Is màirg nach lùbadh an glùn!

Is chi thu ard-ioghnadh Chuith-Fhràing,
Le bhaidealan aibheiseach mòr,—
'San Stòrr cho cas le bhinneinean glas,
Eadar do shealladh 'sna neòil.

Translated—

There frowns the dark Coruisg,
  Which made the great Wizard wonder,
Even Voltaire might heve worshipped there,
  Methinks, in the time of thunder!

There towers the wild Quiraing,
  With its battlements grim and high,
And the mighty Stòrr, with its pinnacles hoar,
  Standing against the sky!

If these lofty pinnacles had tongues to speak, what tales might they relate of the many bloody frays and desperate struggles that took place at their bases in the days of yore. No doubt the aborigines of this and the surrounding Isles had early to defend themselves against the incursions of foreign enemies. The aboriginal people, according to tradition, were a mixture of the ancient Caledonians, or Picts, and the Albanaich, or first settlers of what is now known as the Kingdom of Scotland. The general character of the original population must have been considerably changed by the influx of the Scandinavian enemies, under the command of their sovereigns, the Vikingr, or piratical Kings from Denmark, Norway, and Sweden. These Scandinavian rovers appeared on the east coast of England about the year 785, and a hundred years before they obtained a footing in the Western Isles, which they overcame after much hard fighting, and added them to the Crown of Norway. The Islesmen had great cause to deplore the barbarities of their new oppressors. They destroyed their "cills," or places of worship, which the

The Feuds of the Clans

Culdees had erected some centuries before, and caused desolations and ravages of the most sweeping description in every quarter. Even still, tradition makes mention of the scenes of desperate fights with their piratical foes from the north, although the coasts were well fortified with strong "Dùns," or fortresses, the ruins of which are still distinctly visible. It would be needless, in the meantime, to attempt making mention of the succession of Vikingr, or Kings of the Isles, who reigned therein for several hundreds of years; in short, up to the beginning of the twelfth century, when the powerful dynasty of MacDhòmhnuill, or the Lords of the Isles, had their origin. MacDhòmhnuill was also designated as "Righ nan Eilean," that is, King of the Isles. This great and warlike family sprung from Somerled, Lord of Argyle, and were for a succession of centuries justly renowned for their many achievements and military prowess. At the beginning of the twelfth century, Olave the Red, King of Man, extended his dominion over all the Hebride Isles. He was succeeded by Godred the Black, and one of his daughters, Ragnhildis, was married to Somerled, King of the Isles, in 1140. From this marriage, therefore, sprung the celebrated dynasty, so well known in the history of our Kingdom as the Lords of the Isles.

The original population of the Hebride Isles, whether Pictish or Scottish, in the reign of Kenneth MacAlpine, must have been materially changed by the perpetual inroads and settlements of the warlike Scandinavians. During the two hundred years that intervened from the time of Harold Harfager to that of Olave the Red, the Western Isles were all along the scenes of wars and bloody engagements with their northern invaders. This change in the population must have been perceptible among all classes, but particularly so in the higher ranks, from the natural tendency of invaders to make their possessions more secure by means of matrimonial alliances with the aboriginal natives. That such was the case is well known from the patronimical names of the inhabitants in subsequent ages. It has, therefore, come to pass that at this early date Celts and Scandinavians became amalgamated, and, as it were, of one blood.

It cannot well be ascertained to what extent this mixture was carried, but it would appear that the Celtic race must have predominated, from the fact that the Celtic tongue entirely prevailed, with the exception of the names of localities, which are almost altogether Scandinavian.

Having shortly spoken of the inhabitants of the Western Isles as we find them in the beginning of the twelfth century, I will now briefly allude to the rise, progress, and fall of the powerful dynasty of the Lords of the Isles, and the more so from the circumstance that the influence of that warlike sept extended itself in diversified ramifications throughout not only the Western Isles, but over the length and breadth of Scotland. Before entering on the consideration of any of the feuds that disturbed the peace of the Highlands and Islands, it would be well to consider that the history of this portion of Scotland naturally divides itself into three distinct periods. The first part may embrace its early history and the rise and fall of the great lordship of the Isles; the second part may relate to the various feuds which arose after the forfeiture of that lordship to the time of James VI., by whose exertions the rebellious clans became more loyal and obedient to the national laws; and the third part may embrace an account of the strenuous exertions of many of the clans to support the House of Stuart, which exertions increased in energy in proportion as the hopes of that unfortunate family became more desperate. It is more immediately to the second part of this interesting but complicated history that we would direct your attention, wherein we see the origin and development of the sovereignty claimed by the Lords of the Isles.

It has been already mentioned that the Lords of the Isles had sprung from Somerled, Lord of Argyle, who was known by the appellation of "Somhairle MacGhillebride na h-uàmha," that is, "Somerled, the son of Gillbride of the cave," so called from his having concealed himself in a cave in Morvern during the invasion of the coast by the Scandinavians. In the year 1158, Somerled invaded the Isle of Man with a fleet of fifty-three ships, routed Godred, the King, and laid the whole island waste. By this time Somerled's power over all the Western Isles became so great that Malcolm IV., then King of Scotland, became so alarmed for the safety of his kingdom that he could get no rest. On various occasions Somerled made himself grievously obnoxious to his majesty, and in 1164 he declared open war against his sovereign. With a view to accomplish his rebellious plots, he assembled a numerous army from Ireland, Argyle, and the Northern Isles, sailed up the Clyde with one hundred and sixty galleys well manned, landed his forces near Renfrew, and threatened to make a conquest of all Scotland. Here, according to the ancient annals, Somerled was killed. It is related that he was betrayed and assassinated in his tent, when his troops, in great confusion, retreated to the Isles. It would fill volumes to trace out and record the various septs which sprung from the descendants of Somerled, such as the MacIans of Ardnamurchan, the MacIans of Glenco, the MacRuàiridhs, the MacDonalds of Clan Ranold and Glengarry, the MacDonalds of Keppoch, and many others. John, the first Lord of the Isles, the lineal

The Feuds of the Clans

descendant of Somerled, lived under the reigns of David II. and Robert II., and married Amie, heiress of the MacRuàiridh of Gormoran. He divorced that lady, by whom he had three sons—John, Godfrey, and Ranold. He subsequently married Margaret, daughter of Robert, High Steward of Scotland, by whom he had other three sons—Donald, John, and Alexander. At the death of King David II., the High Steward ascended the throne by the title of Robert II., so that the King had become the father-in-law of John, first Lord of the Isles. This event added much to John's power and influence, and particularly so as he received a royal charter for the lands of Gormoran, regardless of the claims of the first wife's sons, to whom those lands lawfully belonged. Godfrey, the eldest son by the first marriage, resisted these unjust proceedings, and endeavoured to retain his possessions by the power of the sword. The first Lord died at Ardtornish Castle, and was buried with great splendour at Iona. Donald, the eldest son of the second marriage, then became the second Lord of the Isles, and married Mary Leslie, who afterwards became Countess of Ross, in whose right he became the first Earl of Ross of his family. Out of this event a rebellion arose of such a formidable nature as to threaten a dismemberment of the Kingdom of Scotland. The cause of this rebellion, which resulted in the desperate battle of Harlaw, arose as follows. Walter Leslie succeeded to the Earldom of Ross in right of his Lady, Euphemia Ross, who was daughter of that house. Of this marriage there were two children, a son and a daughter. Alexander, the son, succeeded his father in the Earldom, and Mary became the wife of Donald, Lord of the Isles. Alexander married a daughter of the Duke of Albany, then Governor of Scotland, and son of King Robert II. The only family of this marriage was a daughter, who, being weakly both mentally and physically, became a nun, and resigned the Earldom of Ross in favour of her uncle, John Stuart, Earl of Buchan, to the prejudice of Donald, Lord of the Isles, who supposed himself the nearest heir in right of Mary Leslie, his wife. He consequently claimed his right, but finding the Governor, who thought him already too powerful a subject, not inclined to do him the justice he expected, he immediately raised an army of fully 10,000 men within his own Isles, and put himself at their head. His soldiers were fully equipped with bows and arrows, battle-axes, dirks, and swords. He made a rapid descent on the mainland, and burst like a torrent on the disputed territories, carrying everything before him. He was boldly attacked at Dingwall by Angus Dubh Mackay of Farr, but Angus was soon repelled, and most of his men were left dead on the field. He daily recruited his forces, by the way, from the Isles, was determined to put Aberdeen in flames, and to recruit his resources with its spoils. He set his army in order on his arrival at Inverness, marched through the counties of Nairn and Moray, committed great excesses at Strathbogie and the Garioch, and set on fire hundreds of hamlets on the lands of Mar. The appearance, however, of a well-equipped army, under the command of the Earl of Mar, allayed the terrors of the Aberdonians. Mar was powerfully assisted by many Lords and gallant Knights from the Angus and Mearns, and from other southern districts of Scotland. Marching on the village of Inverury, he descried the Highland army close to a village named Harlaw, on the banks of the Ury, near its entrance into the Don. He saw that he had to contend with tremendous odds, but, trusting to the bravery of his leaders, and to the dauntless courage of his steel-clad knights, he resolved to try his fate. He bravely stood at the head of his army, and so did the Lord of the Isles, who was encouraged by many warlike chieftains, such as the MacIntoshes, the Macleans, and the different septs of the Clan Dòmhnuill. It was a moment of dreadful suspense. At length the battle commenced by the setting up of terrific yells and shouts by the Highlanders, who "scrogged" their bonnets, and, battle-mad, rushed like fiends upon the bristling ranks of the enemy. The knights, under Sir James Scrymgeour, received the attack of the Highlanders with much firmness and bravery. They carefully levelled their spears, raised their battle-axes, and hewed down many of the impetuous Islesmen before them. Sweeping forward, they cut their way through the thick columns of the stern Highlanders, carrying destruction and death at every blow. The carnage was dreadful. Still, the brave Islesmen stood fast and firm, and poured in hundreds around Sir James and his gallant knights, to whom no alternative now remained but speedy victory or death; but, alas! the latter fell to their lot. The disastrous result of this battle was the most sweeping misfortune that ever came over the chief families in Buchan, Aberdeen, Angus and the Mearns, and the provinces around. Several of the families became extinct in the male line. Leslie of Balquhain and his six sons fell in battle. To give an idea of the terrible carnage of that day, the following were found among the slain, viz.:—Sir Alexander Ogilvy and son, Sir Robert Maul of Panmure, Sir Thomas Murray, Sir William Abernethy of Salton, Sir Alexander Irvine of Drum, Sir Alexander Straiton of Lauriston, Sir Robert Davidson, Provost of Aberdeen; five hundred of Aberdeen burgesses, and all the principal gentlemen of Buchan. The Highlanders left nearly a thousand of their brave men on the field, including several chiefs and men of distinction.

The bloody battle of Harlaw was fought on 24th July, 1411, and it is difficult to determine on which side the victory lay. Tytler says of it that, "From the ferocity with which it was contested, and the dismal spectacle of civil war and bloodshed exhibited to the country, it appears to have made a deep impression on the national mind. It fixed itself in the music and the poetry of Scotland. A march called 'The Battle of Harlaw' continued to be a popular air down to the time of Drummond of Hawthornden, and a spirited ballad on the same event is still repeated, describing the meeting of the armies, and the deaths of their chiefs, on the battle-field of Harlaw."

In the autumn of the same year, the Duke of Albany, then Regent of Scotland, raised a new army, marched in person at the head of it to the north, seized the Castle of Dingwall, took possession of the lands of Ross, and was determined to subdue the Lord of the Isles. Next season hostilities were renewed, but Donald of the Isles deemed it prudent to surrender his claim to the Earldom of Ross, and to become a vassal to the Scottish Crown.

Speaking of bards and their warlike effusions, it is well known that the Highland chieftains were always accompanied by their bards when they went down to the field of strife, in order to inspire the soldiers with courage. We have a beautiful specimen of this in the war-song of Gaul in the fourth book of Fingal. "Go," said the King of Morven to Ullin, "go, Ullin; go, my aged bard! Remind the mighty Gaul of battle, remind him of his fathers; support the yielding fight, for the song enlivens war." But of the "Brosnachadh-catha," or war-song of the Highlanders, perhaps the most remarkable on record, and certainly so in the Gaelic language, is that of the bard of the Clan Dòmhnuill—Lachlan Mòr MacMhuraich Albanaich. This bard was present at the battle of Harlaw, where he sung this extraordinary war-song to rouse his clan to the highest pitch of enthusiasm before entering on the bloody fray. The poem is 464 years old, and consists of 338 lines. It is a specimen of poetry curious for its alliteration and force. It has a part for every letter of the Gaelic alphabet, and every part consists of vocables commencing with that letter. It shows the

The Feuds of the Clans

copiousness of the language in epithets, seeing that the number poured out under each letter is almost incomprehensible. The bard must have had a wonderful knowledge of the idioms of his native tongue, and nothing less so of the genius of the warlike tribe that he addressed. He almost exhausted the adverbial epithets of his mother-tongue for the purpose of infusing the spirit of true heroism into the breasts of his warlike clan.

I may give a few lines of this interesting poem for the amusement of such as understand it, and of such as understand it not.

He begins with the letter "A," and says:—

Leagaibh orra:—   A.
     A Chlanna Cuìnn, cuimhnichibh,
     Cruas a'n am na h-iarghuill,
     Gu h-arinneach, gu h-arronnach,
     Gu h-àrach, gu h-allonta,
     Gu h-athlamh, gu h-arronta,
     Gu h-allmhara, gu h-arachtach—
     Gu h-anmharach, gu h-aòininntinneach,
     Gu h-armeineach, gu h-anamanta, &c.

Leagaibh orra:—   B.
     Gu beotha, gu barrail,
     Gu brighmhor, gu buàdhach,
     Gu borbanta, gu buànfheargach,
     Gu builleach, gu buìllsgeanach,
     Gu borb, gu beothail,
     Gu béumlannach, gu béumbhuilleach
     Gu bunanta, gu béumach
     Gu beachdaidh, gu béucach, &c.

The Feuds of the Clans

Leagaibh orra:—

C.

Gu calma, gu curanta,
Gu crodha, gu crùadalach,
Gu cruàidhlamhach, gu corrghleusach,
Gu colganta, gu cathmhor,
Gu ceannasach, gu cùramach,
Gu cràobhach, gu cliùiteach,
Gu claoidh-bhuilleach, gu colgarra,
Gu cruaidhbhuilleach, gu casbheumach, &c.

Leagaibh orra:—

D.

Gu dian, gu dùr,
Gu dàsanach, gu deaghfhulangach,
Gu dàna, gu discir,
Gu diònganta, gu dichoisgte,
Gu déinnteach, gu dlubhuilleach,
Gu deàrglamhach, gu dòruinneach,
Gu dòiligh, gu dolùbaidh,
Gu drochmheinneach, gu dubhailceach, &c.

And so on with all the letters of the alphabet, but concludes the long poem with these thirteen graphic lines :—

Gu ùr-labhrach, ùr-làmhach, neartmhor,
Gu coisneadh na câth-làrach,
Ri brùidhne 'ur biùbhaidh,
A Chlanna Chùinn chéud-chathaich,
Si nis uair bhur n-aithneachaidh,
A chuileanan chonfhadach,
A bheirichean bunanta,
A leoghainnean làn-ghasda,
Aon-chonnaibh iarghuilleach
De laochaibh chrodha, churanta,
De Chlannaibh Chùinn chéud-chathaich,
A Chlanna Chùinn cùimhnichibh,
Cruas a'n àm na h-iarghuill.

Niel Macdonald, commonly called "Nial MacMhuraich, and his son Lachlan, were the last of the Clan Ranold family bards, and of the long succession of poets who recorded the illustrious deeds of the clan. Niel Macdonald, who was the fourteenth in lineal descent from Lachlan Mhòr who composed the song at Harlaw, was possessed of some learning, and could write Gaelic well. He kept the records of his clan in Gaelic, wrote their history, and commemorated their talents and prowess in poetic strains. But besides recording what related to the family, he had written volumes of ancient poetry, such as pieces by Ossian, as well as by other ancient bards. It may be interesting to know that, in order to throw more light on these matters, a solemn declaration was made in Gaelic by Lachlan, the bard's son, in presence of the gentlemen afternamed, and said declaration was transmitted to Mr. Henry Mackenzie when composing the Highland Society's Report on Ossian.

I may give a translation in English of this declaration, made in the Island of Barra, on 9th August, 1800.

24   The Feuds of the Clans

TRANSLATION FROM THE GAELIC.

"In the house of Patrick Nicolson at Torlum, near Castle Burgh, in the shire of Inverness, on the 9th day of August, 1800, compeared, in the 59th year of his age, Lachlan, son of Niel, son of Lachlan, son of Niel, son of Donald, son of Lachlan, son of Niel Mòr, son of Lachlan, son of Donald, of the surname of MacVuirich, before Roderick MacNeil, laird of Barra, and declared that, according to the best of his knowledge, he is the 18th in descent from Muireach, whose posterity had officiated as bards to the family of Clanranold, and that they had from that time, as the salary of their office, the farm of Staoiligary, and four pennies of Drimisdale, during fifteen generations; that the sixteenth descendant lost the four pennies at Drimisdale, but that the seventeenth descendant retained the farm of Staoiligary for nineteen years of his life. That there was a right given them over these lands as long as there should be any of the posterity of Muireach to preserve and continue the genealogy and history of the Macdonalds, on condition that the bard, failing of male issue, was to educate his brother's son, or representative, in order to preserve their title to the lands, and that it was in pursuance of this custom that his own father, Niel, had been taught to read and write history and poetry by Donald, son of Niel, son of Donald, his father's brother.

"He remembers well that works of Ossian, written on parchment, were in the custody of his father as received from his predecessors; that some of the parchments were made up in the form of books, and that others were loose and separate, which contained the works of other bards besides those of Ossian.

"He remembers that his father had a book, which was called the *Red Book*, made of paper, which he had from his predecessors, and which, as his father informed him, contained a good deal of the history of the Highland clans, together with part of the works of Ossian. That none of these books are to be found at this day because when they (his family) were deprived of their lands they lost their alacrity and zeal. That he is not certain what became of the parchments, but thinks that some of them were carried away by Alexander, son of the Rev. Alexander Macdonald, and others by

Ronald, his son, and he saw two or three of them cut down by tailors for measures. That he remembers well that Clanranold made his father give up the *Red Book* to James Macpherson from Badenoch; that it was near as thick as a Bible, but that it was longer and broader, though not so thick in the cover. That the parchments and *Red Book* were written in the hand in which the Gaelic used to be written of old, both in Scotland and Ireland, before people began to use the English hand in writing Gaelic; and that his father knew well how to read the old hand. That he himself had some of the parchments after his father's death, but that, because he had not been taught to read, and had no reason to set any value upon them, they were lost. He says that none of his forefathers had the name of Paul, but that there were two of them who were called Cathal.

"He says that the *Red Book* was not written by one man, but that it was written from age to age by the family of Clan Mhuirich, who were preserving and continuing the history of the Macdonalds and of other heads of Highland clans.

The Feuds of the Clans

"After the above declaration was taken down, it was read to him, and he acknowledged it was right in the presence of Donald Macdonald of Balronald, James Macdonald of Garyhelich, Ewan Macdonald of Griminish, Alexander Maclean of Hoster, Mr. Alexander Nicolson, Minister of Benbecula, and Mr. Allan MacQueen, Minister of North Uist, who wrote this declaration.

(Signed) "LACHLAN (X) MACMHUIRICH."
"RODERICK MACNEILL, J.P."

The remarkable statement made by Mr. Campbell of Isla, in which he attributed the authorship of the Ossianic poetry to Mr. Macpherson, is no less ludicrous than bold. It is a rash statement which goes in the face of all external and internal evidence on the subject, and shows the truth of the old maxim—"*Nihil tum absurdum est, quod non dicitur ab aliquis philosophorum.*" There are ample proofs that Macpherson was furnished by parties here and there in the Highlands and Islands with manuscripts and fragments of these poems, as may be seen from the Highland Society's voluminous report, from

Dr. Clerk's learned dissertation on the subject, and from several other sources. The assertion that Macpherson composed these poems, or translated them from the English into Gaelic, is enough to cause such as really know the language to smile with contempt. The language of these poems is so elegant, so exquisite, so unique, and so different in its vocables and phraseology from any modern dialect of the tongue, that I believe no man in the present age could have composed them. Whether the productions are Ossian's or not, they are undoubtedly very old, and must have preceded the establishment of Christianity in the country. The absence in these poems of any allusions to husbandry, or to the arts and sciences, except those of war and of the chase, are strong proofs of their antiquity. On the other hand, the mention of shades and of ghosts, as well as of such animals—now extinct in Scotland—as the wolf, the elk, the reindeer, strongly corroborates the same fact. Anyone like Macpherson who might now attempt to pawn such poetry on the world as his own (but there is no proof that Macpherson ever did it) would soon betray the cloven foot by making some incidental reference to something existing in modern times. Besides, Macpherson's knowledge of Gaelic is alleged not to have been very profound, and such would appear from several passages in his translation, wherein it would seem that when he was ignorant of the meaning of an epithet he translated it by substituting a meaning of his own. I may here allude to a communication which Professor Blackie lately sent to "Nether Lochaber," the talented correspondent of the *Inverness Courier*. That communication was a letter from Mrs. Heugh of Alderly, a lady now in the ninety-sixth year of her age, but still in possession of all her faculties. In that letter she states that she knew Captain Morrison, who, being a good Gaelic scholar, went along with James Macpherson in his tour to the Hebrides to collect the Ossianic poetry. Captain Morrison told her, about the beginning of this century, that he accompanied Macpherson to Skye and to others of the Western Isles, and in course of conversation she heard him say that Macpherson was no more capable of composing these poems than he was of creating the Isle of Skye or of writing the prophecies of Isaiah! And undoubtedly Captain Morrison was perfectly correct.

There is nothing surprising in Mr. Campbell's not finding in the present day a scrap of Macpherson's Ossian among the Highlanders. The wonder would be if he could find it. For the last seventy or eighty years the customs and manners of the Highlanders are entirely changed. The order of the bards in chieftains' families has become extinct. It was their province and delight to rehearse the tales and songs of olden times, and it was likewise the delight of the youth in Highland families to spend their evening pastime in chanting these poems, and in vieing with each other who could repeat most of them. These times are gone. The hardships and depressing circumstances to which the Highlanders have been exposed tended to stamp out their social amusements, such as tales and traditions, the singing of warlike songs, the recitation of ancient poetry, and such like. And the fact is that their boat-songs, their reaping-songs, and their love-songs are all but extinct and lost.

The Feuds of the Clans 31

But speaking of the long line of bards in the family of Clanranold, I may mention that there was another distinguished bard in later times, who sung the praises of his clan in Lochaber. I allude to John Macdonald, commonly called "Ian Lòm" or "Ian Mànndach." He was of the Keppoch family, and was a great politician as well as a poet. He was born in the reign of Charles I., and enjoyed a pension from Charles II. In 1663 the young heir of Keppoch and his brother were murdered by their cousins, and John was instrumental in getting the murderers punished. Ample vengeance was taken on them in the most cruel manner. They were seized and beheaded at a fountain still pointed out in Lochaber to tourists as "Tobar nan ceann," or "The fountain of the heads."

John, although no soldier, was present at the bloody battle of Inverlochy, between Montrose and Argyle, in 1645. He was a keen Jacobite, and was asked by Alexander Macdonald, son of "Coll ciotach," who acted as second in command under Montrose, if he would join them in the battle? "No," said the bard, "but if you do your duty well to-day,

I will do mine in singing your praise to-morrow." He viewed the fight from the battlements of Inverlochy Castle, and next day he composed a song in which he luxuriated like a fiend on the anticipated music of the widows and orphans of the Campbells weeping and clapping their hands in bitter grief for their fallen husbands and fathers! In admiration of this distinguished bard, Mr. Charles Fraser Mackintosh erected a beautiful sculptured monument over his grave in Dun-aingeal, in the braes of Lochaber. The monument was executed by our promising townsmen, the Davidson Brothers, in Academy Street.

Exactly twenty years after the battle of Harlaw, and 214 years before the already-described battle between Montrose and Argyle, Inverlochy was the scene of another desperate and bloody engagement. In consequence of the battle of Harlaw, King James I. was determined to restore order, and for this purpose he held a Parliament at Inverness in the year 1427, and the Lord of the Isles and the other great Highland chiefs were summoned to attend it. On their arrival in the town, upwards of forty of them were seized by his Majesty and confined in separate prisons. The most notorious of them were brought to trial, condemned, and executed. The majority of them, however, were liberated after certain periods of imprisonment, and it is very remarkable that among these was the Lord of the Isles. He, however, severely felt the indignity he had suffered, and was determined on revenge. He lost no time in calling together his adherents in Ross and the Isles, and with ten thousand men he laid waste the Crown lands near Inverness, and burned the town itself to ashes. On the King becoming aware of this, he hastily collected his troops, and by forced marches at the head of his army, he overtook the rebels at Lochaber. On beholding the Royal standard, the Clan Chattan and Clan Chameron, two potent tribes that first supported the Earl of Ross, went over to the cause of the King. His Majesty thus strengthened, immediately attacked and routed the rebels, and pursued them so hotly that their leader was glad to sue for peace. "James, however," as an eminent historian tells us, "sternly refused to enter into a negotiation with his rebellious subject on any other footing than that of an unconditional surrender, and returned to his capital, after having given strict orders to his officers that every effort should be made to apprehend the fugitive Earl. The latter at length, driven to despair by the activity of his pursuers, adopted the resolution of throwing himself on the mercy of his sovereign. Upon the eve of a solemn festival this haughty nobleman presented himself before the King, who, with the Queen and Court, were assembled in the church at Holyrood. He was clothed only in his shirt and drawers; he held his naked sword by the point in his hand; and with a countenance and manner in which destitution and misery were strongly exhibited, he fell upon his knees, and surrendering his sword, implored the Royal clemency. His life was spared, but he was committed to close ward in the castle of Tantallon, under the charge of William, Earl of Angus. While the Earl of Ross was still in prison, the Royal forces which, under the Earls of Mar and Caithness, occupied Lochaber, were surprised and routed by a powerful body of the clans, under the leadership of Domhnull Balloch, full cousin of the Earl of Ross. A desperate battle was fought at Inverlochy, in which the Earl of Caithness and many of the Royal troops were killed, and the Earl of Mar severely wounded." (A.D. 1431.)

One hundred and thirteen years after this bloody engagement, another battle was fought at Inverlochy between the Frasers of Lovat and the Macdonalds of Clan Ranold. This contest was terrible. It began with the discharge of arrows at a distance, but when their shafts were spent, both parties rushed into close combat, and, attacking each other furiously with their two-handed swords and axes, a dreadful carnage ensued. It was the month of July, 1544, and such was the heat of the day and of the strife, that the combatants threw off every vestige of clothing to their shirts, in which they fought like men frantic with fury. Hence the battle was called "Blàr nan léin"—the "Battle of the Shirts." By this destructive fight the Clan Fraser became nearly extinct. James Fraser of Foyers and four common soldiers were the only survivors of this bloody conflict!

In close vicinity to the town of Inverness, a desperate battle was fought at Clachnaharry, in the year 1333, between the Clan Chattan and the Munroes of Fowlis. The cause of the battle was this. John Munro of Fowlis, when returning that year with a band of his retainers from Edinburgh, was insulted at Strathardle, in Perthshire. While resting at night, the owner of the field where they lay cut off the tails of their horses. Munro, determined on revenge, made all possible haste to Ross-shire, selected about 400 of his most powerful retainers, returned to Strathardle, devastated the place, killed many of the natives, and carried off all their cattle. On passing homeward through Moy, Mackintosh, the chief, having had an old grudge to Munro, demanded half the spoil, which Munro absolutely refused to give, and proceeded on his journey. Mackintosh, determined to enforce compliance, immediately collected his clansmen, pursued Munro, and overtook him at Clachnaharry, where a bloody engagement took place. Mackintosh had great cause to repent of his rashness, for he and most of his men were slain in the conflict. The locality of this desperate skirmish is commemorated by a large column erected on the top of the rock by the late Mr. Duff of Muirtown. Clachnaharry signifies the "Watchman's Stone," on which, in ancient times, the Magistrates of Inverness had a guard stationed to give notice of any hostile approach from the north.

As to the system of clanship, or chieftainship, on which volumes might be written, I have no time to enter. Perhaps there is nothing more remarkable in the political history of any country than the succession of the Highland chiefs, and the long and uninterrupted sway which they held over their followers. The people were divided into small tribes over all the Highlands, and each tribe had its chief, its badges, its war-cries, and its tartan or battle-dress. The chieftains held the power of life and death in their own hands. The consequence was that the authority of the King was generally disregarded. "His mandates," as General Stewart says, "could neither stop the depredations of one clan against another, nor allay their mutual hostilities." This system, then, by repudiating the authority of the sovereign, and of the laws, prevented the clans from ever coming to any general terms of accommodation for settling their differences. The consequence was that their feuds were interminable, their quarrels endless, and their country for centuries the theatre of petty warfare and bloodshed. How formidable, therefore, were the chieftains at the head of their followers, who counted every cause just and honourable which their chief approved of, who were ever ready to take the field at his command, and who never refused to sacrifice their lives in defence of his person or of his fame. Now, against such men, animated with enthusiasm and often with blind superstition, a king contended with great disadvantage. Yes, and that cold service which money purchases and which authority extorts, was not an equal match for the burning ardour and zeal of the Highlanders, who deemed it their chief end to live and to die in the cause of their feudal lord!

Innumerable were the causes out of which feuds originated, and innumerable the feuds that did originate and end in bloodshedding from the most trifling causes. Insult has been at the root of many a desperate fray, and insult to a chief was deemed as a personal affront to all his followers, and was resented accordingly.

The Feuds of the Clans

By the system of clanship a warlike spirit was cherished, and young chieftains were held in esteem by their clan exactly in proportion to the extent of their desire to cherish a military or peaceable disposition. If they revenged an insult by killing some of the insulting party, they would be lauded and heartily esteemed for giving such proofs of future bravery, but if they allowed the insult to pass unavenged, either from cowardice or terror, they would become universally despised, and would receive neither countenance nor respect from their clan.

In ancient times each clan had generally a fixed meeting-place, where they held their councils of war, and that meeting-place was usually the Castle or residence of the chief. When an emergency arose for an immediate meeting, the "crànn-taraidh," or "fiery cross," was instantly called into requisition. It consisted of a piece of wood or pole half burnt, then dipped into the blood of a goat or lamb, and having at times a stained flag attached to it. Every chieftain had several of these significant beams of alarm in his possession to enable him to despatch them in every direction. When required, therefore, the messenger set off with it at full speed, and delivered it to the first man he met with at the nearest hamlet. He, in turn, ran to the next hamlet and delivered it there, and so on until it passed through all the hamlets of the chieftain's territories in a few hours, and his vassals instantly assembled. Should any one able to bear arms refuse to obey the call of this mute, blood-stained messenger of slaughter, he would instantly be put to death!

Sir Walter Scott, in the "Lady of the Lake" (canto v., ix), has beautifully described the gathering of the clan at the call of the chief. He says:—

> . . . He whistled shrill,
> And he was answered from the hill;
> Wild as the scream of the curlew;
> From crag to crag the signal flew;
> Instant through copse and heath arose
> Bonnets, and spears, and bended bows,
> On right, on left, above, below,
> Sprung up at once the lurking foe ;
> From shingles grey their lances start,
> The bracken bush sends forth the dart,
> The rushes and the willow wand
> Are bristling into axe and brand,
> And every tuft of broom gives life
> To plaided warrior armed for strife.

The Feuds of the Clans 41

Considering the greatness of the number, the variety, and the complication of Highland feuds from the early periods of clanship, it would be impossible on an occasion of this kind to give an account of even one out of every hundred of them. There is hardly a locality or district in the Highlands and Islands but has been the scene of some bloody feudal rencontre. How endless were the disputes between the clans. There were bloody feuds between the Munroes and the Clan Chattan, between the Clan Chattan and the Camerons, between the Clan Chattan and the Mackays, and between the Mackays and the Rosses. Mr. C. F. Mackintosh lately alluded to the long protracted feud between Mackintosh and Lochiel, relative to which a great number of influential gentlemen held a council in vain on Tomnahurich Hill, in order to reconcile the warlike combatants. What commotions were in the Western Isles from the insurrections of the Macdonalds against the Mackenzies, the Mackays, the Macleans, the Macdougalls, the Camerons, the Campbells, the Frasers, the Gunns, and the different septs of the Macleods! The very names of Macdonald of Sleat, Clanranold, Glengarry, Keppoch, and Glencoe, indicate battles and bloodshedding! Sutherland, Caithness, and Ross-shire were the scenes of serious invasions, and the fields of many fierce engagements. The Macgregors and Colquhouns fought a desperate battle in Glenfruin in 1603, when the latter party were routed with the loss of two hundred men. So very indignant was Colquhoun, Laird of Luss, at this disaster, that he misrepresented the whole affair to King James VI. a little before he quitted Scotland to commence his reign as sovereign of Great Britain. Luss sent up to Edinburgh upwards of 200 bloody shirts of his slain vassals to show the King the cruelty of the heartless invaders, so that his Majesty, without hearing both sides of the question, grew exceedingly incensed at the Macgregors, proclaimed them rebels, and interdicted all his lieges from harbouring a single soul of them. They were hunted like partridges on the mountains by the Earl of Argyle and his deceitful retainers. Heavy fines were imposed on all who sheltered the unfortunate clan. The fines were punctually levied, and as punctually pocketed by Argyle as recompense for his services against the maligned and persecuted Clan Gregor. Then it was that this powerful but unfortunate sept could sing the plaintive song—

> We're landless, landless, landless, Gregarach.

During these feuds, many of the deeds done were painfully heartrending and cruel. For example—owing to a feud betwixt the Clanranolds of Uist and the Macleods of Dunvegan, the Uist men landed at Waternish, on the south-west side of Skye, on a Sabbath morning. On their arrival, they set fire to the church at Trumpan, being full of the Macleods at divine service. The ruins of the church are still entire. All were burned to death but one woman, who escaped and caused the fiery cross to be set abroad. The Macleods soon assembled—sooner, indeed, than the invaders could enter their galleys and sail away. A fierce battle ensued, wherein all the Clanranold men fell. The slain were ranged behind a dyke near the scene of the fight, on the lands of Ardmore, and the stones and turf of the dyke were hurled upon the dead bodies to bury them. Their bones may be picked up there among the stones to this day. The battle was called "Blàr Milleadh Gàraidh," or "Blàr-Bhaternish," by which name a beautiful piobaireachd was then composed by MacCrimmon.

The island of Eigg was inhabited then by a tribe of the Macdonalds, and the Macleods of Skye, in order to be revenged of the cruel catastrophe at Trumpan, set sail for Eigg to cut off the Clanranolds there root and branch. The Eigg men, seeing the galleys of the enemy approaching from Skye, hid themselves, being several hundreds in number, in a large cave on the shore of the island, which is entered by a narrow opening, but is wide and capacious within. They were soon discovered by footprints in the snow, and as the Macleods could not approach them in the cave, they piled furniture, turf, straw, and such combustibles as they could lay hold of, at the mouth of the cave, set fire to the whole, and suffocated every living soul within it. When I saw the cave forty-five years ago, cart-loads of skulls and other human bones lay scattered about within it.

About the year 1590, Dòmhnull Gòrm Mòr of Sleat discovered that his near relative,

"Uisdean MacGhilleaspuig Chléirich," who had been acting as his factor in Uist, had been laying secret plots against him. Uisdean had built a castle or fortress for himself at Peinduin, near Kingsburgh, in Skye, which had neither door nor window at the sides, but was lighted from the roof, where there was an entrance which was arrived at by a ladder that would be drawn up when the party got upon the top of the fortress. The ruin of this castle is still pretty entire. When Uisdean understood that his chief had discovered the plot, he departed to the Long Island to conceal himself. He was a robust, powerful man, who required a strong party to seize him. At length, however, he was apprehended, and carried prisoner to Duntulm Castle, where he was cast into a deep, vaulted dungeon (still in existence), and fed with salt beef, but no water. He died of thirst, uttering fearful screams that resounded through the halls of the castle. His remains were buried in "Reilig Mhòr Mhic Dhòmhnuill"—"the Macdonald's cemetery," near Flora Macdonald's grave, in Kilmuir Churchyard, but about twenty years thereafter his skull and thigh-bones were exhumed by one of the family, who did not think them worthy of the place, and were thrown into a recess in the walls of the old church, where they lay dry and polished for nearly two centuries. The old church was taken down, and my father, then minister of that parish, buried the bones in the churchyard, in the autumn of 1823.

I may mention one other remarkable feudal battle, and then cease from taxing your patience by making but few more remarks. In 1601, Domhnull Gòrm Mòr of Sleat married Margaret, sister of Sir Roderick Macleod, commonly called "Rory Mòr" of Dunvegan, but "for some displeasure or jealousy conceived against her," he sent her back to her brother. The lady was blind of an eye, but to show all the indignity in his power, her husband procured a one-eyed horse for her, a one-eyed valet, and a one-eyed terrier, and when the one-eyed party arrived at Rory Mòr's castle, he had two good eyes to see the insult that was given him by the chief of the Macdonalds. Sir Rory was determined on revenge, and immediately left Skye to solicit the aid of friendly chiefs in the south, and particularly so that of the Earl of Argyle, in order to be avenged of the chief of the Macdonalds. In his absence, Donald of Sleat assembled his forces, and invaded the territories of Rory Mòr. Alexander, a brother of Rory Mòr, hastily collected all the fighting men of his clan, and encamped at the base of the Cullin Hills. Next day the combatants met, and fought desperately from the rising to the setting of the sun. The victory, after great slaughter on both sides, fell to Domhnull Gòrm Mòr. He eventually divorced Margaret Macleod, and married a sister of Kenneth Mackenzie of Kintail. About forty or fifty years ago, a bagpipe chanter of great calibre was found embedded in moss in the ravine where the battle was fought. The chanter was in an excellent state of preservation, and is, I believe, in the possession of John M'Kinnon, Esq., Kyle Cottage, Skye.

So much, then, for Highland Feuds, and for all such internal disturbances as marred the peace and prosperity of the Highlands and Islands for a long series of years. Happily, these things have come to an end. The transition state of the Gael is now past. Those feudal periods are gone wherein it was deemed that the spirit of revenge was the true spirit of heroism and victory. Their steadfast allegiance to their chiefs, their hearts' desire to support them in their differences with hostile tribes, and their readiness to encounter an enemy on the battle-field regardless of all danger, only showed the sincerity and devotedness of their hearts. But since then, those native principles of fidelity which characterised the people of these mountains and glens, have fortunately diverged into other channels, and have been called forth, not any longer for the support of lawless chieftains, but for the interest of their sovereign, their liberty, and their laws. The change is a mighty one, and a blessed one. The Highlanders have their language, their poetry, and their music still left, and need I say that much is done in the present day to support and maintain, nay, if possible, to perpetuate these things for ages to come. On the other hand, their native bravery never left them. They fought in their battles fierce as lions before the invention of muskets, powder, and shot. Even since then, when danger was imminent, they cast away their firearms and had recourse to other instruments, which they considered more destructive and deadly. Even so late as the battle of Killiecrankie, it is said that the clans earnestly entreated the Viscount Dundee not to engage in person, and told his Lordship that their method of fighting was quite different to that of regular troops. They requested of him to consider that should he be killed, King James's interest might be lost in Scotland. But nothing would dissuade Dundee from engaging at the head of his troops, and he was soon slain. Seeing this, the Highlanders, animated afresh, threw away their plaids, haversacks, and all other loose encumbrances, and marched boldly and deliberately in their shirts and kilts to face their opponents. They grasped their fusils, swords, dirks, and targets, rushed furiously down the hill, dashed through the line of the enemy with fearful carnage, and in an instant completely discomfited General Mackay and his officers. It is said that few such strokes were ever given in Europe as were laid on that day by the Highlanders! Many of Mackay's soldiers were cut down through the skull and neck to the very breast, and many others had their scalps cut off above the ears like nightcaps. Bodies and crossbelts were severed at one blow, while pikes and scimitars were broken like willow wands!

> Full well their trenchant swords with cleaving blows,
> Avenged the iron hail-showers of their foes;
> But, ah! though all had 'scaped, since Clavers fell,
> Our much-wronged king might bid his throne farewell.

In short, the bravery and loyalty of the Highlanders, ever since the happy termination of the several civil wars that so long distracted the peace of our nation, are well known, and will ever remain as monuments to their credit to the remotest generations. How nobly did our Highland regiments ever distinguish themselves in all quarters of the wide world!

> All places they visit their valour proclaim,
> Which exists to all ages, of wonder a theme;
> Yea, the world shall with pleasure it henceforth record,
> While great actions delight can impart or afford!
>
> Oft with glory return'd, out of fields from afar,
> The stout champions of sharp, hardy strokes, and of war,
> Who prefer before luxury, ease, or applause,
> To defend their sweet liberty, country, and laws!
>
> By exploits full of hazard, they often were tried;
> No retreat was allowed by their courage and pride;
> For the custom of fathers renown'd in their life,
> Must not change in the offspring engag'd in the strife.

TOUCHING THE DESCRIPTION OF SUTHERLAND.

OUR Scottish writers have hitherto erred in describing the situation of Sutherland; for it hath Caithness toward the east and north-east; Strathnaver toward the north; Assint toward the west; Ross toward the south and south-west; and the German Sea toward the south, south-east, and east. Sutherland, in the Irish language, is called Cattey, and the people Cattigh. Cattey did contain sometime all the region lying betwixt Tayne and Dungesby, being divided in the midst by a mountain called Mond, or Ord, which runneth from the south sea to the north sea: and the country which is now called Catteyness, was first so named, as the ness or promontory of Cattey stretching itself eastward from the hill Ord. This is the opinion of one Andrew, Bishop of Catteyness. And in the old English writers (such as Hoveden, Walsinghame, and others) it is always written Catteynes: so that Boethius faileth in drawing the etymology of Catteyness from Catus (the proper name of a man) and **ness**; which doubtless proceeded from the **ignorance of the Irish language.**

THE FEUDS OF THE CLANS.

THE CONFLICT OF DRUMILEA.

ABOUT the year of God 1031, in the days of Malcolm the Second, King of Scotland, the Danes and Norwegians, under the conduct of Olanus and Enetus, seated themselves in the north parts of Scotland, and took the Castle of Nairn, where they became very strong; from thence they sent divers companies of soldiers into the neighbouring provinces, not only to prey, but likewise to seat themselves there, as they should find occasion and opportunity. Olanus did then send a strong company to invade the provinces of Ross and Sutherland, and to destroy the inhabitants; which Allan, Thane of Sutherland, perceiving, he assembled his countrymen, and the inhabitants of Ross, with all diligence, and fought a battle at

Creich, in Sutherland, against the Danes and Norwegians, who had then come from Nairn, in Moray, and had landed in the river of Portnacouter, which divideth Ross from Sutherland. After a long and doubtful fight, the Danes were overthrown, and chased to their vessels. The monument whereof remains there unto this day, at a place called Drumilea before Creich.

THE CONFLICT OF EMBO.

About the year of God 1259, the Danes and Norwegians did land at the ferry of Unes, with a resolution to invade Sutherland and the neighbouring provinces, against whom William, Earl of Sutherland, made resistance, and encountered with them betwixt the town of Dornoch and the ferry at Unes, at a place called Embo. After a sharp conflict the Danes are overthrown, their general slain, with many others, and the rest chased to their ships; in memory of which a monument of stone was there erected, which was called Righ-Chrois, that is, the king's or general's cross, which, together with divers burials, is there to be seen at this day.

THE CONFLICT OF BEALACH-NA-BROIGH.

About the year of God 1299, there was an insurrection made against the Earl of Ross by some of the people of that province, inhabiting the mountains, called Clan Iver, Clantall-wigh, and Clan-Leawe. The Earl of Ross made such diligence that he apprehended their captain, and imprisoned him at Dingwall, which so incensed the Highlanders that they pursued the Earl of Ross's second son at Balnagown, took him and carried him along prisoner with them, thinking thereby to get their captain relieved. The Munroes and the Dingwalls, with some other of the Earl of Ross's dependers, gathered their forces, and pursued the Highlanders with all diligence; so, overtaking them at Bealach-na-Broig, betwixt Ferrindonnell and Lochbrime, there ensued a cruel fight, well fought on either side. The Clan Iver, Clantall-wigh, and Clan-Leawe, were almost all utterly extinguished; the Munroes had a sorrowful victory, with great loss of their men, and carried back again the Earl of Ross's son. The Laird of Kildun was there slain, with seven score of the surname of Dingwall. Divers of the Munroes were slain in this conflict; and among the rest, there were killed eleven of the house of Fowlis, that were to succeed one another, so that the succession of Fowlis fell unto a child then lying in his cradle, for which service the Earl of Ross gave divers lands to the Munroes and the Dingwalls.

THE CONFLICT OF CLACHNAHARRY.

About the year of God 1341, John Munro, tutor of Fowlis, travelling homeward on his journey from the south of Scotland, towards Ross, did repose himself by the way, in Strathardale, betwixt Saint Johnstone and Athole, where he fell at variance with the inhabitants of that country, who had abused him, which he determined to revenge afterward. Being come to Ross, he gathered together his whole kinsmen, neighbours, and followers, and declared unto them how he had been used, and craves their aid to revenge himself, whereunto they yield. Thereupon he singled out 350 of the strongest and ablest men among them, and so went to Strathardale, which he wasted and spoiled, killed some of the people, and carried away their cattle. In his return home (as he was passing by the Isle of Moy with his prey), Mackintosh, chieftain of the Clan Chattan, sent to him to crave a part of the spoil, challenging the same as due to him by custom. John Munro offered Mackintosh a reasonable portion, which he refused to accept, and would have no less than the half of the whole spoil, whereunto John would not yield. So Mackintosh, convening his forces with all diligence, followed John Munro, and overtook him at Clachnaharry, beside Kessock, within one mile of Inverness. John, perceiving them coming, sent fifty of his men to Ferrindonnell with the spoil, and encouraged the rest of his men to fight. So there ensued a cruel conflict, where Mackintosh was slain with the most part of his company. Divers of the Munroes were also killed, and John Munro left as dead on the field; but after all was appeased, he was taken up by some of the people thereabout, who carried him to their houses, where he recovered of his wounds, and was afterwards called John Back-lawighe, because he was mutilated of an hand.

The Feuds of the Clans

THE CONFLICT OF CLAN CHATTAN AND CLAN KAY.

Robert III. in the year 1396 sent Lindsay, Earl of Crawford, and Dunbar, Earl of Murray, to suppress a violent contest between the Clans Chattan and Kay, who being numerous, bold, and barbarous, mutually plundered and murdered each other. They, fearing lest they should not effect the matter without much bloodshed, had recourse to policy, viz.:—That thirty on each side should enter themselves as champions for their respective clans, and decide their differences by the sword, without being allowed any other weapon. This proposal was agreed to on both sides. The King and his nobility were to be spectators of the combat. The conquered clan were to be pardoned for all their former offences, and the conquerors honoured with the royal favour. The North Inch of Perth, a level spot, so called from being partly surrounded by water, was to be the scene of action; but upon the mustering the combatants, it was found that one of them, belonging to the Clan Chattan, had absented himself through fear, and could not be found. It was proposed to balance

The Feuds of the Clans 59

the difference by withdrawing one of the Clan Kay; but none of them could be prevailed upon to resign the honour and danger of the combat. After various other expedients failing, one Henry Wynd, a smith, though no way connected with either clan, offered to supply the place of the absentee, upon his receiving a French crown of gold (about the value of seven shillings and sixpence) which was accordingly paid him. The encounter was maintained on both sides with inconceivable fury; but, at length, by the superior valour, strength, and skill of Henry Wynd, victory declared herself for the Clan Chattan. Of them no more than ten, besides Wynd, were left alive, and all dangerously wounded. The combatants of the Clan Kay were all cut off, excepting one, who remained unhurt, threw himself into the Tay, and escaped to the opposite bank.

THE CONFLICT OF TUITEAM-TARBHACH.

The year of God 1406, this conflict was fought at Tuiteam-Tarbhach, in the south-west part of Sutherland, as it marches with Ross. Upon this occasion, Angus Mackay of Strathnaver married Macleod of the Lews' sister, by whom he had two sons, Angus Dow and Rory Gald. Angus Mackay dying, he leaves the government of his estate and children to his brother Uistean Dow Mackay. Macleod of the Lews, understanding that his sister, the widow of Angus Mackay, was hardly dealt withal in Strathnaver by Uistean Dow, he takes journey thither to visit her, with the choicest men of his country. At his coming there, he finds that she is not well dealt withal, so he returned home malcontent, and in his way he spoiled Strathnaver and a great part of Brae-Chat in the height of Sutherland. Robert, Earl of Sutherland, being advertised thereof, he sent Alexander Murray of Cubin, with a company of men, to assist Uistean Dow in pursuing Macleod, and to recover the prey. They overtake Macleod at Tuiteam-tarbhach, as he and his company were going to the west sea, where Alexander Murray and Uistean Dow invaded them with great courage. The fight was long and furious, rather desperate than resolute. In the end they recovered the booty, and killed Macleod with all his company. This conflict gave name to the place where it was fought, being then called Tuiteam-tarbhach, which signifieth a plentiful fall or slaughter, and is so called unto this day.

THE CONFLICT OF LON-HARPASDAL.

The year of God 1426, Angus Dow Mackay, with his son Neil, enters Caithness with all hostility, and spoiled the same. The inhabitants of Caithness assembled with all diligence, and fought with Angus Dow Mackay at Harpasdal, where there was great slaughter on either side. Whereupon King James I. came to Inverness, of intention to pursue Angus Dow Mackay for that and other such like enormities. Angus Dow, hearing that the King was at Inverness, came and submitted himself to the King's mercy, and gave his son Neil in pledge of his good obedience in time coming, which submission the King accepted, and sent Neil Mackay to remain in captivity in the Bass; who, from thence, was afterwards called Neil Wasse Mackay.

THE CONFLICT OF DRUIMNACOUB.

The year of God 1427, Thomas Mackay (otherwise Macneil), possessor of the lands of

Creich, Spanzedell, and Polrossie, in Sutherland, had conceived some displeasure against the laird of Freswick, called Mowat, whom Thomas Macneil did eagerly pursue, and killed him near the town of Tain, in Ross, within the Chapel of St. Duffus, and burnt also that chapel unto which this Mowat had retired himself as to a sanctuary. The King hearing of this cruel fact, he causes to proclaim and denounce Thomas Macneil rebel, and promised his land to any that would apprehend him. Angus Murray (the son of Alexander Murray of Cubin, above-mentioned), understanding the King's proclamation, had secret conference with Morgan and Neil Mackay, brethren to this Thomas. Angus offered unto them, if they would assist him to apprehend their brother, that he would give them his own two daughters in marriage, and also assist them to get the peaceable possession of Strathnaver, which they did claim as due to them, and (as he thought) they might then easily obtain the same, with little or no resistance at all, seeing that Neil Wasse Mackay (the son of Angus Dow) lay prisoner in the Bass, and Angus Dow himself was unable (by reason of the weakness of his body at that time) to withstand them. Morgan Mackay and Neil Mackay do condescend and yield to the bargain; and presently, thereupon, they did apprehend their brother, Thomas, at Spanzedell, in Sutherland, and delivered him to Angus Murray, who presented him to the King, at whose command Thomas Macneil was executed at Inverness; and the lands of Polrossie and Spanzedell, which he did possess, were given to Angus Murray for this service; which lands his successors do possess unto this day. Angus Murray, for performance of his promise made to Neil and Morgan Mackay, gave them his two daughters in marriage. Then Angus deals with Robert, Earl of Sutherland, that he might have his attollerance to convene some men in Sutherland, therewith to accompany his two sons-in-law to obtain the possession of Strathnaver. Earl Robert grants him his demand; so Angus having gathered a company of resolute men, he went with these two brethren to invade Strathnaver. Angus Dow Mackay, hearing of their approach, convened his countrymen, and, because he was unable himself in person to resist them, he made his bastard son (John Aberigh) leader of his men. They encountered at Druimnacoub, two miles from Tongue — Mackay's chief dwelling-place. There ensued a cruel and sharp conflict, valiantly fought a long time, with great slaughter, so that, in the end, there remained but few alive of either side. Neil Mackay, Morgan Mackay, and their father-in-law (Angus Murray), were there slain. John Aberigh, having lost all his men, was left for dead on the field, and was afterwards recovered; yet he was mutilated all the rest of his days. Angus Dow Mackay, being brought thither to view the place of the conflict, and searching for the dead corpses of his cousins, Morgan and Neil, was there killed with a shot of an arrow, by a Sutherland man, that was lurking in a bush hard by, after his fellows had been slain. This John Aberigh was afterwards so hardly pursued by the Earl of Sutherland, that he was constrained, for safety of his life, to flee into the Isles.

The Scottish historians, in describing this conflict, do mistake the place, the persons, and the fact; and do quite change the whole state of the history. For the person—Angus

Dow Mackay of Strathnaver is by some of them called Angus Duff, and by others, Angus Duff of Strathern. For the place—they make Angus Duff of Strathern to come from Strathern (some say from Strathnaver), to Moray and Caithness, as if these shires did join together. For the fact—they would have Angus Duff to come for a prey of goods out of Caithness and Moray, which two shires do not march together, having a great arm of the sea interjected betwixt them, called the Moray Firth, and having Ross and Sutherland betwixt them by land. But the truth of this conflict and the occasion thereof I have here set down.

THE CONFLICT OF RUAIG-SHANSAID.

The year of God 1437, Neil Wasse Mackay, after his release out of the Bass, entered Caithness with all hostility, and spoiled all that country. He skirmished with some of the inhabitants of that province at a place called Sanset, where he overthrew them, with slaughter on either side. This conflict was called Ruaighanset, that is, the Chase at Sanset. Shortly thereafter Neil Wasse died.

The Conflict of Blar-Tannie.

About the year of God 1438, there fell some variance betwixt the Keiths and some others of the inhabitants of Caithness. The Keiths, mistrusting their own forces, sent to Angus Mackay of Strathnaver (the son of Neil Wasse), entreating him to come to their aid, whereunto he easily yielded; so Angus Mackay, accompanied with John Mor MacIan-Riabhaich, went into Caithness with a band of men, and invaded that country. Then did the inhabitants of Caithness assemble in all haste, and met the Strathnaver men and the Keiths at a place in Caithness called Blair-tannie. There ensued a cruel fight, with slaughter on either side. In the end the Keiths had the victory, by the means chiefly of John Mor MacIan-Riabhaich (an Assynt man), who was very famous in these countries for his manhood shown at this conflict. Two chieftains and leaders of the inhabitants of Caithness were slain, with divers others. This Angus Mackay, here mentioned, was afterwards burnt and killed in the Church of

Tarbat, by a man of the surname of Ross, whom he had often molested with incursions and invasions.

THE CONFLICT OF BLAR-NA-PAIRC.

After the Lord of the Isles had resigned the Earldom of Ross into the King's hands, the year of God 1477, that province was continually vexed and molested with incursions of the Islanders. Gillespick (cousin to Macdonald), gathering a company of men, invaded the height of that country with great hostility ; which, the inhabitants perceiving (and especially the Clan Mackenzie), they assembled speedily together, and met the Islanders beside the river of Conon, about two miles from Brayle, where there ensued a sharp and cruel skirmish. The Clan Mackenzie fought so hardly, and pressed the enemy so, that in the end Gillespick Macdonald was overthrown and chased, the most part of his men being either slain or drowned in the river of Conon; and this was called Blar-na-Pairc.

The Conflicts of Skibo and Strathfleet.

About the same time, Macdonald of the Isles, accompanied with some of his kinsmen and followers, to the number of five or six hundred, came into Sutherland, and encamped hard by the Castle of Skibo, whereupon Neil Murray (son or grandchild to Angus Murray, slain at Druimnacoub) was sent by John, Earl of Sutherland, to resist them, in case they did offer any harm unto the inhabitants. Neil Murray, preceiving them going about to spoil the country, invaded them hard by Skibo, and killed one of their chieftains, called Donald Dow, with fifty others. Macdonald, with the rest of his company, escaped by flight, and so retired into their own country.

Shortly thereafter another company of Macdonald's kin and friends came to Strathfleet in Sutherland, and spoiled that part of the country, thinking thereby to repair the loss they had before received; but Robert Sutherland (John, Earl of Sutherland's brother), assembled some men in all haste, and encountered with them upon the sands of Strathfleet. After a sharp and cruel skirmish, Macdonald's men were overthrown, and divers of them killed.

THE CROWNER SLAIN BY THE KEITHS IN THE CHAPEL OF ST. TAYRE.

About the year of God 1478, there was some dissension in Caithness betwixt the Keiths and the Clan Gunn. A meeting was appointed for their reconciliation, at the Chapel of St. Tayre, in Caithness, hard by Girnigo, with twelve horse on either side. The Crowner (chieftain of the Clan Gunn) with the most part of his sons and chief kinsmen came to the chapel, to the number of twelve; and as they were within the chapel at their prayers, the Laird of Inverugie and Ackergill arrived there with twelve horse, and two men upon every horse; thinking it no breach of trust to come with twenty-four men, seeing they had but twelve horses as was appointed. So the twenty-four gentlemen rushed in at the door of the chapel, and invaded the Crowner and his company unawares; who, nevertheless, made great resistance. In the end the Clan Gunn were all slain, with the most of the Keiths. Their blood may be seen at this day upon the walls within the Chapel of St. Tayre, where they were slain. Afterwards William Mackames (the Crowner's grandchild) in revenge of his grandfather, killed George Keith of Ackergill and his son, with ten of their men, at Drummuie in Sutherland, as they were travelling from Inverugie into Caithness.

The Conflict of Aldicharrish.

The year of God 1487, this conflict was fought; upon this occasion Angus Mackay being slain at Tarbat by the surname of Ross, as I have shown already, John Riabhach Mackay (the son of this Angus), came to the Earl of Sutherland, upon whom he then depended, and desired his aid to revenge his father's death, whereunto the Earl of Sutherland yields, and sent his uncle, Robert

Sutherland, with a company of men, to assist him. Thereupon, Robert Sutherland and John Riabhach Mackay did invade Strathoyckel and Strathcarron with fire and sword; burnt, spoiled, and laid waste divers lands appertaining to the Rosses. The laird of Balnagown (then chief of the Rosses in that shire) learning of his invasion, gathered all the forces of Ross and met Robert Sutherland and John Riabhach at a place called Aldicharrish. There ensued a cruel and furious combat, which continued a long time, with incredible obstinacy; much blood was shed on either side. In the end, the inhabitants of Ross, being unable to endure or resist the enemies' forces, were utterly disbanded and put to flight. Alexander Ross, Laird of Balnagown, was slain with seventeen other landed gentlemen of the province of Ross, besides a great number of common soldiers. The manuscript of Fearn (by and attour Balnagown) names these following among those that were slain. Mr. William Ross, Angus Macculloch of Terrell, John Waus, William Waus, John Mitchell, Thomas Waus, Houcheon Waus.

The Skirmish of Dail-Riabhach.

The year of God 1576, Y Roy Mackay of Strathnaver dying, there arose civil dissension in Strathnaver betwixt John Mackay (the son of Y Roy) and Neil Nawerigh (the said Y Roy's brother). John Mackay excludes his uncle Neil (who was thought to be the righteous heir), and took possession of Strathnaver. Neil, again, alleging that his nephews John and Donald were bastards, doth claim these lands, and makes his refuge of John, Earl of Caithness, of whom he did obtain a company of men, who were sent with Neil's four sons to invade Strathnaver. They take the possession of the country from John Mackay, who, being unable to resist their forces, retires to the Clan Chattan to seek their support, and leaves his brother Donald Mackay to defend the country as he might. Donald, in his brother John's absence, surprised his cousin-german under silence of the night at Dail-Riabhach, and killed two of his cousins (the sons of Neil Nawerigh) with the most part of their company. Thereafter, Neil Nawerigh came and willingly surrendered himself to his nephews John and Donald, who caused apprehend their uncle Neil, and beheaded him at a place called Clash-nan-ceap in Strathnaver.

THE CONFLICT OF TORRAN DUBH.

Adam Gordon, first of that surname, Earl of Sutherland, having married Elizabeth Sutherland, heiress of that country, took journey to Edinburgh, the year of God 1517, to dispatch some affairs there, which did concern the settling of his estate, leaving the commandment of the country, in his absence, to Alexander Sutherland (base brother to his wife Elizabeth) and to John Murray of Abirscors; which John Mackay of Strathnaver, understanding (having now appeased his civil discords at home, by the death of his uncle Neil) this occasion, in the very change of surnames in Sutherland, to try if he could gain anything by spoiling that country; and thereupon assembling together all the forces of Strathnaver, Assynt, and Eddrachillis, with all such as he could purchase out of the west and north-west isles of Scotland, invades the country of Sutherland with all hostility, burning and spoiling all before him. The inhabitants of Sutherland do speedily convene together with all the parts of the country; and so, under the conduct of Alexander Sutherland, John Murray, and William Mackames, they rencounter with John Mackay and his company at a place called Torran Dubh, beside Rogart, in Strathfleet, where there ensued a fierce and cruel conflict. The Sutherland men chased John Mackay's vanguard, and made them retire to himself where he stood in battle array; then did he select and choose a number of the ablest men in all his host, and, with these, he himself returned again to the conflict, leaving his brother Donald to conduct the rest, and to support him as necessity should require; whereupon they do begin a more cruel fight than before, well fought on either side. In end, after long resistance, the Sutherland men obtained the victory; few of these that came to renew the fight escaped, but only John Mackay himself, and that very hardly. Neil MacIan-MacAngus of Assynt was there slain, with divers of his men. There were 216 of the Strathnaver men left dead in the field, besides those that died in the chase. There were slain of Sutherland men 38. Not long

thereafter John Mackay sent William and
Donald, two brethren, with a company of men,
to invade John Murray, with whom they met at
a place called Loch-Sallachie, in Sutherland.
After a sharp skirmish, both the chieftains of
the Strathnaver men were slain, with divers of
their men, and the rest put to flight; neither
was the victory pleasing to John Murray, for he
lost there his brother, called John Roy-Murray.
Thus continued the inhabitants of these countries infesting one another with continued spoils,
until the year of God 1522, that Alexander
Gordon (Earl Adam's eldest son) overthrew
John Mackay at Lairg, and forced him to
submit himself to Earl Adam; unto whom
John Mackay gave his band of manrent and
service, dated the year of God 1522.

THE CONFLICT OF ALLTAN-BEATH.

Donald Mackay of Strathnaver, having succeeded his brother, John, taketh the occasion
upon the death of Adam, Earl of Sutherland
(who left his grandchild, John, young to
succeed him) to molest and invade the in-

habitants of Sutherland. He came, the year of God 1542, with a company of men to the village of Knockartoll, burnt the same, and took a great prey of goods out of Strathbrora. Sir Hugh Kennedy of Griffen Mains dwelt then in Sutherland, having married John, Earl of Sutherland's mother, after the death of his father, Alexander, Master of Sutherland. Sir Hugh Kennedy being advertised of Mackay's coming into Sutherland, he advises with Hutcheon Murray of Abirscors, and with Gilbert Gordon of Garty, what was best to be done. They resolve to fight the enemy; and so having gathered a company of men, they overtook Mackay, unawares, beside a place called Alltan-Beath, where they invaded him suddenly; having passed his spies unseen. After a little skirmish the Strathnaver men fled, the booty was rescued, and John MacIan-MacAngus, one of their chieftains, was slain, with divers of the Strathnaver men. Donald Mackay, nevertheless, played the part of a good soldier; for in his flight he killed, with his own hand, one William Sutherland, who most eagerly pursued him in the chase. The inhabitants of Sutherland

and Strathnaver (in regard of Earl John's minority) did thus continually vex one another, until this Donald Mackay was apprehended and imprisoned in the Castle of Fowlis, in Ross, by commandment of the Queen Regent and the Governor, where he continued a good while in captivity.

THE CONFLICT OF GARBHARRY.

The Queen Regent having gotten the Government of Scotland from the Earl of Arran, she made her progress into the North, and so to Inverness, the year of God 1555. Then was Y Mackay (the son of Donald) summoned to compear before the Queen at Inverness, for that he had spoiled and molested the country of Sutherland during Earl John's being in France with the Queen Regent. Mackay refused to compear, whereupon there was a commission granted to John, Earl of Sutherland, against him. Earl John invaded Strathnaver in all hostile manner, and besieged the Castle of Borve, the principal fort of that country, which he took by force, and caused hang the Captain, then demolished the fort. In end, he beset Y Mackay so, on all sides, that he forced him to render himself, and then was delivered by Earl John to Sir Hugh Kennedy, by whom he was conveyed South and committed to ward in the Castle of Edinburgh, where he remained a long space. Whilst Y Mackay staid in captivity, his cousin-german, John Mor Mackay, took upon him the government of Strathnaver. This John Mor taking the occasion of Earl John's absence in the south of Scotland, he invaded Sutherland with a company of the most resolute men in Strathnaver; they burnt the chapel of St. Ninians in Navidell, where the inhabitants of the country, upon this sudden tumult, had conveyed some of their goods; so, having spoiled that part of the country, they retire homeward. The inhabitants of Sutherland assembled together, and followed in all haste under the conduct of MacJames, the Terrell of the Doil, and James MacWilliam. They overtook the Strathnaver men at the foot of the hill called Beinn-mhor, in Berriedale, and invaded them beside the water of Garbharry, where then ensued a cruel conflict, fought with great obstinacy. The Strathnaver men were overthrown and chased; above 120 of them were slain, and some drowned in Garbharry. This is the last conflict that hath been fought betwixt Sutherland and Strathnaver.

THE BURNING OF THE DORNOCH CATHEDRAL.

John, Earl of Sutherland, together with his lady, being poisoned, the year 1567, his son Alexander (being young) succeeded unto him, whose ward and marriage George, Earl of Caithness, had right to, and withal gets the custody of Earl Alexander during the time of his ward; whereat Alexander's most tender friends (and chiefly the Murrays of Sutherland) being grieved, they lay a plot among themselves to convey Earl Alexander from the Earl of Caithness; which they effect, and deliver him to the Earl of Huntly, with whom he stayed until his ward was expired, the year 1573, during which time the Earl of Caithness kept possession of the land; whereupon divers troubles did ensue. The Earl of

Caithness removed the Murrays of Sutherland from their possessions; which, nevertheless, they endeavoured to keep. Hutcheon Murray, with divers of his friends, do possess themselves with the town of Dornoch and the adjacent lands, being formerly possessed by them. The Earl of Caithness sent his son John, Master of Caithness, with a number of men to remove the Murrays from Dornoch. Y Mackay did also accompany the Master of Caithness in his journey. Being come to Dornoch, they besiege the Murrays there; who, for the space of some days, issued forth and skirmished with the enemy. In end, the Master of Caithness burnt the town and the cathedral church, which the inhabitants could not longer defend. Yet, after the town was lost, they kept the Castle, the enemy still assaulting them, but in vain, without any success, for the space of a month. Then, by the mediation of some indifferent friends, they surrendered the Castle, and gave three pledges that, within two months, they should depart from Sutherland; which they did, and retired themselves to the Earl of Huntly, with whom they stayed until the expiring of the Earl Alexander's ward; at which time they recovered their ancient possessions. Notwithstanding that the Murrays had retired themselves as they had promised, yet they were no sooner departed but the pledges were beheaded.

During the time that the Sutherland men stayed with the Earl of Huntly, they served him in his wars against the Forbeses, and chiefly at Crabstaine, where they did good service against the foot supply that was sent by the Regent to assist the Forbeses. This burning of Dornoch and of the Cathedral church happened in the year of God 1570. The next year following (which was 1571), George, Earl of Caithness, became jealous of some plots which his eldest son John, Master of Caithness, and Y Mackay of Strathnaver had contrived against him, and thereupon apprehended his son John, whom he imprisoned closely at Girnigo, where he died after seven years' captivity. Y Mackay, perceiving that John, Master of Caithness, was imprisoned by his father, he retired home into Strathnaver, and died within six months thereafter, the same year of God 1571.

THE CONFLICTS OF ALLT-GAMHNA AND LECKMELM.

The year of God 1585, George, Earl of Caithness, married the Earl of Huntly's sister; at which time, by Huntly's mediation, the Earls of Sutherland and Caithness were reconciled. It was then concluded among them that the Clan Gunn should be pursued and invaded by the Earls of Sutherland and Caithness, because they were judged to be the chief authors of the troubles which were then like to ensue; and to this effect it was resolved that two companies of men should be sent by the Earls of Sutherland and Caithness against such of the Clan Gunn as dwelt in Caithness, thereby to compass them, that no place of retreat might be left unto them, which was done. The Earl of Sutherland's company was conducted by John Gordon of Backies and James MacRorie; the Earl of Caithness's company was conducted by his cousin, Henry Sinclair—a resolute gentleman. It happened that Henry Sinclair and his company rencountered first with the Clan Gunn, who were now assembled together at a hill called Bingrime, and with them was William Mackay (brother to Hugh Mackay of Strathnaver, and nephew to this Henry Sinclair that led the Caithness men) who was accompanied with some Strathnaver men. Now were the Clan Gunn advertised of this preparation made against them; and no sooner were they in sight of one another but they prepared both for the fight, which was begun without fear or delay on either side. The Clan Gunn, although inferior in number, yet they had the advantage of the hill, by reason of which the Caithness men came short with their first flight of arrows; by the contrary, the Clan Gunn spared their shot until they came hard by the enemy, which then they bestowed among them with great advantage. Then ensued a sharp conflict, at a place called Allt-gamhna, where Henry Sinclair was slain with 120 of his company, and the rest chased and put to flight, who had all been destroyed had not the darkness of the night favoured their flight. Which, coming to the ears of John Gordon, James MacRorie, and Neil MacIan-MacWilliam, who had the conduct of the Earl of Sutherland's men, they pursued the Clan Gunn, and followed them to Lochbroom, in the height of Ross, whither they had fled; and then, meeting with them, they invade them at a place called Leckmelm. After a sharp skirmish, the Clan Gunn were overthrown, and chased, 32 of them slain, and their Captain, George, wounded and taken prisoner, whom they carry along with them unto Dunrobin, and there they deliver him unto Alexander, Earl of Sutherland. This happened in the year of God 1586.

TROUBLES IN THE WESTERN ISLES IN THE YEAR 1586.

This commotion in the Western Isles of Scotland did arise, at this time, betwixt the Clan Donald and the Clan Lean, upon this occasion. Donald Gorme Macdonald of Sleat, travelling from the Isle of Skye to visit his cousin, Angus Macdonald of Kintyre, landed with his company on an island called Jura or Duray, which partly appertaineth to Maclean, partly to Angus Macdonald; and by chance he landed in that part of the island which appertaineth to Maclean, being driven thither by contrary winds; where they were no sooner on shore, but two outlaws, Macdonald Herrach and Hutcheon Macgillespick (who were lately fallen out with Donald Gorme) arrived also with a company of men; and understanding that Donald Gorme was there, they secretly took away, by night, a number of cattle out of that part of the island which appertaineth to Maclean; and so they retire again to the sea; thereby thinking to raise a tumult against Donald Gorme, by making the Clan Lean to believe that this was done by Donald Gorme's men, who, lying at a place called Inverknockbhric, were suddenly invaded unawares, under silence of the night (neither suspecting nor expecting any such matter) by Sir Lauchlan Maclean and his kin, the Clan Lean, who had assembled their whole forces against him. Maclean and his people killed, that night, above 60 of the Clan Donald; Donald Gorme himself, with the residue, escaped, by going to keep in a ship that lay in the harbour. Angus Macdonald of Kintyre hearing of this lamentable accident fallen out betwixt his brother-in-law, Maclean (whose sister he had married), and his cousin,

Donald Gorme, he taketh journey into Syke to visit Donald Gorme, and to see by what means he could work a reconciliation betwixt him and Maclean for the slaughter of Donald Gorme's men at Inverknock-bhric. After Angus had remained a while in Syke with his cousin, he taketh journey into Kintyre; and in his return he landed in the Isle of Mull, and went to Duart (Maclean's chief dwelling-place in Mull) against the opinion of his two brothers, Coll and Ronald, and of his cousin, Ronald Macdonald, who all persuaded Angus to the contrary; desiring him to send for Maclean, and so, to declare unto him how he had sped with his cousin, Donald Gorme, and how far he was inclined to a reconciliation; but Angus trusted so much in his brother-in-law, Sir Lauchlan Maclean, that he would not hearken unto their counsel; whereupon his two brothers left him, but his cousin, Ronald Macdonald, accompanied him to Duart, where Angus at first was welcomed with great show of kindness; but he, with all his company, were taken prisoners by Sir Lauchlan Maclean, the next day after their arrival, Ronald Macdonald escaping, and that very hardly. Angus was then detained in captivity, until he did renounce his right and title to the Rhinns of Islay, which property appertaineth to the Clan Donald, and had been by them given in possession for their personal service. Angus was forced to yield, or there to end his days; and for performance of what was desired, Angus gave his eldest son, James, and his brother, Ronald, as pledges, to remain at Duart, until Maclean should get the title of the Rhinns of Islay made over to him; and so, the pledges being delivered, Angus got his liberty.

Angus Macdonald, receiving the wrong at Maclean's hand, besides that which his cousin Donald Gorme had received at Inverknockbhric, he went about, by all means, to revenge the same; and the better to bring this purposed revenge to pass, he used a policy by a kind of invitation, which was thus: Maclean having got the two pledges into his possession, he taketh journey into Islay, to get the performance of what was promised unto him, leaving Ronald, one of the pledges, fettered in a prison at his house of Duart, in Mull, and carrying his nephew James (the son of

Angus) and the other pledge along with him in his voyage. Being arrived in the Isle of Islay, he encamped at Ellan-lochgorm, a ruinous fort lying upon the Rhinns of Islay. Thereupon Angus Macdonald took occasion to invite Maclean to come to Mullintrae, or Mulndrhea (a dwelling-place which Angus had well furnished in the Isle of Islay), seeing he was better provided of all kind of provision there than Maclean could be; earnestly intreating him to lie at his house, where he should be as welcome as he could make him; that they should make merry so long as his provision could last, and when that was done, he would go with him. For this custom the Islanders have, that when one is invited to another's house, they never depart so long as any provision doth last; and when that is done they go to the next, and so from one to one, until they make a round from neighbour to neighbour, still carrying the master of the former family with them to the next house. Moreover, all the Islanders are of nature very suspicious, full of deceit and evil intention against their neighbours, by whatsoever way they may get them destroyed; besides this, they are so cruel in taking revenge that neither have they regard to person, time, age, nor cause, as you may partly see in this particular. Sir Lauchlan Maclean's answer to Angus Macdonald's messenger was that he durst not go to him, for mistrust. Angus then replied that he needed not to mistrust, seeing he had his son and his brother pledges already, whom his friends might keep in their custody until his return; and that, for his own part, he did intend nothing against him, but to continue in all brotherly love and affection towards him. Maclean, hearing this, seemed to be void of all suspicion, and so resolves to go to Angus's house; he carried with him James Macdonald, the pledge (his own nephew, and the son of Angus), whom he kept always in his custody, thereby to save himself from danger, if any injury should be offered unto him. He came to Mullintrea, accompanied with 86 of his kinsfolk and servants, in the month of July, 1586, where at the first arrival, they were made welcome with all courtesy, and sumptuously banqueted all that day; but Angus, in the meantime, had premonished all his friends and well-wishers within Islay to be at his house the same night at nine o'clock; for he had concluded with himself to kill them all the very first night of their arrival, and still concealed his purpose, until he found the time commodious, and the place proper. So Maclean, being lodged with all his men in a long house that was somewhat distant from other houses, took to be with him his nephew James, the pledge before mentioned, with whom he never parted; but within an hour thereafter, when Angus had assembled his men, to the number of 300 or 400, he placed them all in order about the house where Maclean then lay. Angus himself came and called upon Maclean at the door, offering him his reposing drink, which was forgotten to be given him before he went to bed. Maclean answered that he desired none for that time. Although, said Angus, it be so, yet it is my will that thou arise and come forth to receive it. Then began Maclean to suspect, and so did arise, with his nephew James betwixt his shoulders, thinking, that if present killing was intended against him, he would save himself as long as he could by the boy. The boy, seeing his father with a bare sword, and a number of his men in like manner about him, cried, with a loud voice, for mercy to his uncle, which was granted, and Maclean immediately removed to a secret chamber till the next morning. Then called Angus to the remnant within, so many as would have their own lives to be saved, that they should come forth (Macdonald Herrach, and another, whom he named, only excepted); obedience was made by all the rest, and these two only fearing the danger, refused to come forth; which Angus perceiving, he commanded incontinent to put fire to the house; which was done, so that the two men were pitifully burnt to death. This Macdonald was the author of these troubles; the other was a very near kinsman to Maclean, and of the eldest of his sirname, renowned both for counsel and manhood.

After that, the report of Maclean's taking came to the Isle of Mull, Allan Maclean, and some others of the Macleans, caused a rumour to be spread in Islay, that Ronald (the brother of Angus Macdonald, and the other pledge which he had given to Maclean) was slain at Duart, in Mull, by Maclean's friends; which false report was raised by Allan Maclean, that thereby Angus Macdonald might be moved to kill his prisoner, Sir Lauchlan Maclean, and so Allan himself might succeed to Sir Lauchlan; and, indeed, it wrought this effect, that how soon the report came to Angus's ears that his brother Ronald was slain, he revenged himself fully upon the prisoners: for Maclean's followers were by couples beheaded the days following, by Coll, the brother of Angus.

The report of this fact at Mullintrae was carried to the Earl of Argyll, who immediately assembled his friends to get Maclean out of Angus's power; but, perceiving that they were not able to do it, either by force or fair means, they thought necessary to complain to the King. His Majesty directed charges to Angus, by a herald of arms, commanding him to restore Maclean into the hands of the Earl of Argyll; but the messenger was interrupted, and the haven port stopped, where he should have taken shipping towards Islay, and so he returned home; yet with exceeding travel made by Captain James Stewart, Chancellor of Scotland, and many straight conditions granted by Maclean to Angus, Maclean was at last exchanged for Ronald, the brother of Angus, and the pledge before mentioned; and for performance of such conditions as Maclean did promise to Angus, at his delivery, he gave his own son, and the son of Macleod of Harris, with divers other pledges to Angus Macdonald, who thereupon went into Ireland, upon some occasion of business, which Maclean understanding, he invaded the Isle of Islay, and burnt a great part of the same, regarding neither the safety of the pledges, nor his faith given before the friends at his delivery.

Angus Macdonald, returning out of Ireland, did not stir the pledges, who were innocent of what was done unto his lands in his absence; yet, with a great preparation of men and shipping he went into the islands and Tiree appertaining to Maclean, invading these places with great hostility; where, what by fire, what by sword,

and what by water, he destroyed all the men
that he could overtake (none excepted), and all
sorts of beasts that served for domestic
use and pleasure of man; and, finally, came
to the very Ben Mor, in Mull, and there
killed and chased the Clan Lean at his pleasure, and so fully revenged himself of his
former injuries. Whilst Angus Macdonald was
thus raging in Mull and Tiree, Sir Lauchlan
Maclean went into Kintyre, spoiled, wasted,
and burnt a great part of that country;
and thus, for a while, they did continually
vex one another with slaughters and outrages,
to the destruction, well near, of all their
country and people.

In the meantime, Sir Lauchlan Maclean
did entice and train John MacIan, of Ardnamurchan (one of the Clan Donald), to come
unto him unto the Isle of Mull, promising
him that he would give him his mother
in marriage, unto whom the said John
MacIan had been a suitor. John being
come unto Mull, in hope of this marriage,
Maclean yielded to his desire, thinking thereby to draw John MacIan unto his party
against Angus Macdonald. The marriage was

celebrated at Torloisk, in Mull; but the very same night John MacIan's chamber was forced, himself taken from his bed out of Maclean's mother's arms, and eighteen of his men slain, because he refused to assist Maclean against Angus Macdonald. These were (and are to this day) called, in a proverb, "Maclean's nuptials."

John MacIan was detained a whole year in captivity by Maclean; and, at last, was released, in exchange of Maclean's son and the rest of the pledges which Angus Macdonald had in his hands. These two islanders, Angus Macdonald and Maclean, were afterwards written for by the King, and trained unto Edinburgh, the year of God 1591, with promise safely to pass and repass unhurt or molested in their bodies or goods, and were committed both to ward within the Castle of Edinburgh, where they remained not long when they were remitted free, to pass home again, for a pecunial fine, and a remission granted to either of them. Their eldest sons were left as pledges for their obedience in time coming.

THE TROUBLES BETWEEN SUTHERLAND AND CAITHNESS IN 1587-90.

The year of God 1587, there happened some dissension betwixt the Earls of Sutherland and Caithness. Upon this occasion George Gordon of Marle in Sutherland (base son to Gilbert Gordon of Gartie), had done divers attempts and indignities to the Earl of Caithness and his servants, occasioned through the nearness of George Gordon's dwelling-house, which bordered upon Caithness. These insolencies of George Gordon's the Earl of Caithness could not or would not endure; and so assembling a company of men, horse and foot, he comes under silence of the night and invades George Gordon in his own house at Marle. George makes all the resistance he could; and, as they were eagerly pursuing the house, he slays a special gentleman of Caithness, called John Sutherland; therewith he issues out of the house and casts himself into the river of Helmsdale, which was hard by, thinking to save himself by swimming; but he was shot

The Feuds of the Clans

with arrows, and slain in the water. This happened in the month of February, 1587.

Alexander, Earl of Sutherland, took the slaughter of George Gordon in evil part, which he determined to revenge, and thereupon dealt with such of his friends as had credit at Court for the time; by whose means he obtained a commission against the slayers of George Gordon; which being gotten, he sent 200 men into Caithness in February, 1588, conducted by John Gordon of Golspitour, and John Gordon of Backies, who invaded the parishes of Dunbeath and Latheron in Caithness with all hostility, spoiling and burning the same; they killed John, James's son, a gentleman of Caithness, with some others; and this was called Creach-lairn.

No sooner were they returned out of Dunbeath but Earl Alexander, being accompanied by Uistean Mackay (who had been then lately reconciled to his superior, the Earl of Sutherland), entered into Caithness with all his forces, spoiling all before him till he came to Girnigo (now called Castle Sinclair), where the Earl of Caithness then lay. Earl Alexander escaped himself, hard by the town of Wick, which is within a mile of Girnigo. They took the town of Wick with little difficulty, and burnt the same. They besieged the Castle of Girnigo for the space of twelve days, which was well defended by the Earl of Caithness and those that were within. Earl Alexander, perceiving that the Castle could not be obtained without a long siege, sent his men abroad through the county of Caithness to pursue such as had been at the slaughter of George Gordon, if they could be apprehended; so, having slain divers of them, and spoiled the country, Earl Alexander returns again with his host into Sutherland in the month of February, 1588. And this was called Là-na-Creich-Moire.

The Earl of Caithness, to revenge these injuries, and to requite his losses, assembled all his forces in the year of God 1589, and sent them into Sutherland, under the conduct of his brother, the Laird of Murkle, who entered Sutherland with all hostility, and, coming to Strathullie, he slays three tenants of the Earl of Sutherland's in Liriboll, burning the house above them; from Liriboll they march further into the country. The inhabitants of Sutherland, being conducted by Uistean Mackay and John Gordon of Backies, met with the Caithness men at a place called Crissaligh, where they skirmished a little while, with little or no slaughter on either side; and so Murkle retired home into Caithness. In exchange hereof, Alexander, Earl of Sutherland, sent 300 men into Caithness, conducted by John Gordon of Backies, the same year of God 1589, who, entering that county with all hostility, spoiled and wasted the same till he came within six miles of Girnigo, killed above 30 men, and returned home with a great booty. This was called Creach-na-Caingis.

The Earl of Caithness, to repair his former losses, convened his whole forces the year of God 1590. He entered into Sutherland with all hostility, and encamped beside the Backies; having stayed one night there, they returned homeward the next day, driving a prey of goods before the host. By this time some of the inhabitants of Sutherland were assembled to the number of 500 or 400 only, and, perceiving the Caithness men upon the sands of Clentrednal, they presently invade them at a place called Clyne. There ensued a sharp conflict, fought with great obstinacy on either side, until the night parted them. Of the Sutherland men, there were slain John Murray, and sixteen common soldiers. Of the Caithness men, there were killed Nicholas Sutherland (the Laird of Forse's brother), and Angus MacTormoid, with thirteen others. Divers were hurt on either side.

The next morning timely the Earl of Caithness returned with all diligence into Caithness, to defend his own country; for while he was in Sutherland, Uistean Mackay had entered with his forces into Caithness, and had spoiled that country even to the town of Thurso; but, before the Earl of Caithness could overtake him, he returned again into Strathnaver with a great booty.

Thus they infested one another with continual spoils and slaughters, until they were reconciled by the mediation of the Earl of Huntly, who caused them meet at Strathbogie; and a final peace was concluded there, betwixt these parties, in the month of March, 1591. Here ends this book of Sutherland.

The Troubles Between the Earls of Huntly and Moray.

The instruments of this trouble were the Laird of Grant and Sir John Campbell of Calder, knight. The Knight of Calder had spent the most part of his time in Court, where he was familiar with Chancellor Maitland, from whom he received instructions to engender differences betwixt Huntly and Moray; which commission he accomplished very learnedly, and inflamed the one against the other by the Laird of Grant's means. Thus, James Gordon (eldest son to Alexander Gordon of Lismore), accompanied with some of his friends, went to Ballindalloch, in Strathspey, to assist his aunt, the widow of that place, against John Grant, tutor of Ballindalloch, who went about to do her son injury, and to detain her rents from her. James Gordon coming thither, all was restored unto the widow, a small matter excepted; which, not understanding, he would have from the tutor, thinking it a disgrace to him and to his family if his aunt should lose the least part of her due. After some contestation, there was beating of servants on either side; and, being put asunder at that time, James Gordon and his company retired home. Hereupon the family of Lismore do persuade John Gordon (brother to Sir Thomas Gordon of Cluny) to marry the widow of Ballindalloch, which he did. The tutor of Ballindalloch, grudging that any of the surname of Gordon should dwell among them, fell at variance with John Gordon, by the Laird of Grant's persuasion, and killed one of John Gordon's servants; whereat John Gordon was so incensed, and pursued so eagerly the tutor and such of the Grants as would assist, harbour, or maintain him or his servants, that he got them outlawed, and made rebels by the laws of the Kingdom; and, further, he moved his chief, the Earl of Huntly, to search and follow them by virtue of a commission as Sheriff of that shire. Huntly besieges the house of Ballindalloch, and takes it by force the 2nd day of November, 1590; but the tutor escaped. Then began Calder and Grant to work their premeditated plot, and do stir up the Clan Chattan and their

chief, Mackintosh, to join with the Grants;
they persuade also the Earls of Athole and
Moray to assist them against Huntly. They
show the Earl of Moray that how he had a
fit opportunity and occasion to make himself
strong in these north parts, and to make
head against the House of Huntly; that they
and all their friends would assist him to the
uttermost of their power; that Chancellor
Maitland would work at Court to this effect
against Huntly; so that now he should not
slip this occasion, lest afterward he should
never have the like opportunity in his time.
Hereupon the Earls of Moray and Athole,
the Dunbars, the Clan Chattan, the Grants,
and the Laird of Calder, with all their faction,
met at Forres to consult of their affairs,
where they were all sworn in one league
together, some of the Dunbars refusing to
join with them. Huntly, understanding that
the Earls of Moray and Athole did intend to
make a faction against him, assembled his
friends with all diligence, and rides to Forres,
with a resolution to dissolve their Convention.
Moray and Athole, hearing of Huntly's coming
towards them, leave Forres and flee to

Darnaway, the Earl of Moray's chief dwelling-place. The Earl of Huntly follows them thither; but, before his coming, the Earl of Athole, the Lairds of Mackintosh, Grant, Calder, and the Sheriff of Moray had left the house and were fled to the mountains; only the Earl of Moray stayed, and had before provided all things necessary for his defence. Huntly, coming within sight of the house, he sent John Gordon before-mentioned, with some men, to view the same; but John, approaching more hardily than warily, was shot from the house, and slain with a piece by one of the Earl of Moray's servants. Huntly, perceiving the House of Darnaway furnished with all things necessary for a long siege, and understanding also that the most part of his enemies were fled to the mountains, left the house and dissolved his company, the 24th of November, 1590. The Earl of Huntly thereupon hastens to the Court, and doth reconcile himself to Chancellor Maitland, who shortly thereafter (not so much for the favour he bore to Huntly as for the hatred he had conceived against the Earl of Moray for Bothwell's cause), did purchase a commission to Huntly against the Earl of Moray, caring little in the meantime what should become either of Moray or Huntly. The year of God 1591, Huntly sent Allan Macdonuill-Duibh into Badenoch against the Clan Chattan; after a sharp skirmish the Clan Chattan were chased, and above fifty of them slain. Then Huntly sent MacRonald against the Grants, whom MacRonald invaded in Strathspey, killed eighteen of them, and wasted all Ballindalloch's lands. The year of God 1591, the 27th of December, the first raid of the Abbey was enterprised by the Earl of Bothwell; but, failing of his purpose, he was forced to flee away, and so escaped. The Duke of Lennox and the Earl of Huntly were sent into the West with a commission against Bothwell, and such as did harbour him; but Bothwell escaped before their coming. Then took the Earl of Moray his fatal and last journey from Darnaway south to Dunibristle, where he did harbour and recept the Earl of Bothwell. Huntly being now at Court, which then sojourned at Edinburgh, urges Chancellor Maitland for his commission against the Earl of Moray; and, having obtained the same, he takes journey with forty gentlemen from Edinburgh to the Queen's Ferry, and from thence to Dunibristle, where he invades the Earl of Moray. Huntly, before his approach to the house, sent Captain John Gordon (brother to William Gordon, laird of Gight) to desire the Earl of Moray to give over the house and to render himself, which was not only refused, but also Captain John Gordon was deadly hurt by a piece, by one of the Earl of Moray's servants, at his very first approach to the gates; whereupon they set fire to the house and forced the entry. Huntly commanded the Earl of Moray to be taken alive, but the laird of Cluny, whose brother was slain at Darnaway, and the laird of Gight, who had his brother lying deadly wounded before his eyes, overtaking Moray, as he was escaping out of the house, killed him among the rocks upon the seaside. There was also the Sheriff of Moray slain by Innes of Invermarkie, which happened the 7th day of February, 1591. Presently hereupon Huntly returned into the North, and left Captain John Gordon at Inverkeithing until he recovered of his wound, when he was taken by the Earl of Moray's friends and executed at Edinburgh, being scarce able to live one day longer for his wound received at Dunibristle. Sir John Campbell of Calder, Knight, who was the worker and cause of their troubles, and of the miseries that ensued thereupon, was afterwards pitifully slain by his own surname in Argyle.

The Earl of Huntly was charged by the Lord St. Colme (the late slain Earl of Moray's brother) to underly the censure of the law for the slaughter of Dunibristle. Huntly compeared at Edinburgh on the day appointed, being ready to abide the trial of an assize; and, unto such time as his peers were assembled to that effect, he did offer to remain in ward in any place the King would appoint him; whereupon he was warded in the Blackness, the 12th day of March, 1591, and was released the 20th day of the same month, upon security and caution given by him that he should enter again upon six days' warning whensoever he should be charged to that effect.

After the Earl of Moray's slaughter at Dunibristle, the Clan Chattan (who of all that faction most eagerly endeavoured to revenge his death) did assemble their forces under the conduct of Angus Macdonald, William's son, and came to Strathdisse and Glenmuck, where they spoiled and invaded the Earl of Huntly's lands, and killed four gentlemen of the surname of Gordon, among whom was the old Baron of Breaghly, whose death and manner thereof was much lamented, being very aged and much given to hospitality. He was slain by them in his own house, after he had made them good cheer and welcome, never suspecting them, or expecting any such reward for his kindly entertainment, which happened, the first day of November, 1592. In revenge whereof, the Earl of Huntly, having gotten a commission against them, assembled his power and raid into Petty (which was then in the possession of the Clan Chattan), where he wasted and spoiled all the Clan Chattan's lands, and killed divers of them; but, as the Earl of Huntly had returned home from Petty, he was advertised that William Macintosh, with 800 of Clan Chattan, were spoiling his lands of Cabrich; whereupon Huntly and his uncle,

Sir Patrick Gordon of Auchindown, with some few horsemen, made speed towards the enemy, desiring the rest of his company to follow him with all possible diligence, knowing that, if once he were within sight of them, they would desist from spoiling the country. Huntly overtook the Clan Chattan before they left the bounds of Cabrich, upon the head of a hill called Steeplegate, where, without staying for the rest of his men, he invaded them with those few he then had; after a sharp conflict he overthrew them, chased them, killed 60 of their ablest men, and hurt William Mackintosh with divers others of his company.

Shortly afterward the Earl of Huntly convened his forces and went the second time into Petty, causing Alexander Gordon of Abergeldie, Huntly's bailie in Badenoch for the time, bring down his Highlandmen of Lochaber, Badenoch, and Strathdown, to meet him at Inverness, desiring him also, in his journey towards Inverness, to direct some men of Clan Ranald's into Strathspey and Badenoch, to spoil and waste the laird of Grant and Mackintosh's lands, which was done; and afterward Abergeldie and Mac-Ranald, with the Highlandmen, met Huntly at Inverness, from whence (joining altogether) they invaded Petty, where they wasted, burnt, and spoiled all the rebels' lands and possessions, killed a number of them, and then returned home into their countries.

Whilst the North of Scotland was thus in a combustion, the Spanish Blanks were discovered, and Mr. George Carr, Doctor of the Laws, was apprehended in the Isle of Cumbrae, and brought back to Edinburgh, 1592. Afterward, the year of God 1594, the Popish Earls, Angus, Huntly, and Errol, were, at the earnest suit of the Queen of England's ambassador, forfeited at a Parliament held at Edinburgh the penult of May, 1594. Then was the King moved to make the Earl of Argyll, his Majesty's Lieutenant in the North of Scotland, to invade the Earls of Huntly and Errol. Argyll, being glad of this employment (having received money from the Queen of England for this purpose), makes great preparation for the journey, and addresses himself quickly forward; thinking thereby to have a good occasion to revenge

The Feuds of the Clans 111

his brother-in-law, the Earl of Moray's death; so on he went, with full assurance of a certain victory, accompanied with the Earl of Tullibardine, Sir Lauchlan Maclean, and divers Islanders, Mackintosh, Grant, and Clan Gregor, Macneill of Barra, with all their friends and dependers, together with the whole surname of Campbell, with sundry others, whom either greediness of prey or malice against the Gordons had thrust forward in that expedition; in all, above 10,000 men. And, coming through all the mountainous countries of that part of Scotland, they arrived at Ruthven of Badenoch, the 27th of September, the year 1594, which house they besieged, because it appertained to Huntly; but it was so well defended by the Clan Pherson (Huntly's servants) that Argyll was forced to give over the siege and to address himself towards the Lowlands; where the Lord Forbes, with his kin, the Frasers, the Dunbars, the Clan Kenzie, the Irvines, the Ogilvies, the Leslies, the Munroes, and divers other surnames of the North, should have met him as the King's Lieutenant, and so join with his forces against Huntly.

Argyll came thus forward to Drummin, in Strathdown, and encamped hard thereby, the 2nd of October. Huntly and Errol, hearing of this great preparation made against them, lacked neither courage nor resolution; they assemble all such as would follow them and their fortune in this extremity. Errol came unto the Earl of Huntly to Strathbogie with 100 or 120 of resolute gentlemen; and so, having there joined with Huntly's forces, they march forward from thence to Carnburgh, and then to Achindown, with 1500 horsemen, the 3rd of October; parting from Achindown, Huntly sent Captain Thomas Carr and some of the family of Tillieboudie (Gordon), to spy the fields and view the enemy. These gentlemen, meeting by chance with Argyll's spies, killed them all, except one whom they saved and examined, and by him understood that Argyll was at hand. This accident much encouraged the Earl of Huntly's men, taking this as a presage of an ensuing victory; whereupon Huntly and Errol do resolve to fight with Argyll before he should join with the Lord Forbes and the rest of his forces; so they march towards the enemy, who, by

The Feuds of the Clans 113

this time, was at Glenlivet, in the mountains of Strathavon.

The Earl of Argyll, understanding that Huntly was at hand, who (as he believed) durst not show his countenance against such an army, he was somewhat astonished, and would gladly have delayed the battle until he had met with the Lord Forbes; but, perceiving them to draw near, and trusting to his great number, he began to order his battle, and to encourage his people with the hope of prey, and the enemy's small forces to resist them. He gave the commandment and leading of his vanguard to Sir Lauchlan Maclean and to Achinbreck, which did consist of 4000 men, whereof 2000 men were hagbutters. Argyll himself and Tullibardine followed with all the rest of the army. The Earl of Errol and Sir Patrick Gordon of Achindown, accompanied with the Laird of Gight, Bonnietoun Wood, and Captain Carr, led the Earl of Huntly's vanguard, which consisted of 300 gentlemen; Huntly followed them with the rest of his company, having the Laird of Cluny (Gordon), upon his right hand, and Abergeldie upon the left hand;

and, as he began to march forward, he encouraged his men, shewing them that there was no remedy, but either to obtain the victory, or to die with their weapons in their hands, in defence of whatsoever they held dearest in this world.

Argyll, his army being all footmen, and assailed, had the advantage of the ground; for they were arrayed in battle upon the top of a steep, rough, and craggy mountain, at the descent whereof the ground was foggy, mossy, and full of peatpots, exceeding dangerous for horse. Huntly's forces consisted all in horsemen, and were constrained to ride first through the mossy ground at the foot of the hill, and then to ride up against that heathy, rough mountain, to pursue the enemy, who did there attend them. Before that Errol and Achindown gave the first charge, Huntly caused Captain Andrew Grey (now Colonel of the English and Scottish in Bohemia) to shoot three field-pieces of ordnance at the enemy, which bred a confused tumult among them, by the slaughter of MacNeill of Barra, an Islander, and one of the most valiant men of that party.

The Feuds of the Clans 115

Huntly's vanguard, seeing the enemy disordered, presently gave the charge; the Earl of Errol, with the most part of the vanguard, turned their sides towards the enemy, and so went a little about, directly towards Argyll, leaving Maclean and the vanguard upon their left hand, being forced thereto by the steepness of the hill, and the thick shot of the enemy; but Achindown, with the rest of his company, did gallop up against the hill towards Maclean; so that Achindown himself was the first man that invaded the enemy, and the first that was slain by them, having lost himself by his too much forwardness. The fight was cruel and furious for a while. Achindown's servants and followers, perceiving their master fall, raged among their enemies, as if they had resolved to revenge his death, and to accompany him in dying.

Maclean, again playing the part of a good commander, compassed Huntly's vanguard, and enclosed them betwixt him and Argyll, having engaged themselves so far that now there was no hope of retreat; so that they were in danger to be all cut in pieces, if Huntly had not come speedily to their support, where he was in great danger of his life, his horse being slain under him; but being presently horsed again by Invermarkie, he rushed in among the enemies. Thus the battle was again renewed with great fury, and continued two hours. In end, Argyll with his main battle began to decline, and then to flee apace, leaving Maclean still fighting in the field; who, seeing himself thus destitute of succours, and his men either fled or slain, retired in good order with the small company he had about him, and saved himself by flight; having behaved himself in the battle, not only like a good commander, but also like a valiant soldier.

Huntly and his horsemen followed the chase beyond the brook of Aldchonlihan, killing the enemies, till the steepness of the next mountains did stay them, being inaccessible for horsemen. Argyll's ensign was found in the place of battle, and brought back with them to Strathbogie.

The Earl of Argyll lost in this battle his two cousins, Archibald Campbell of Lochnell, and his brother, James Campbell, with divers

The Feuds of the Clans

of Achinbreck's friends, MacNeill of Barra, and 700 common soldiers. Neither was the victory very pleasing to the Earl of Huntly, for, besides that the Earl of Errol, the Laird of Gight, and the most part of all his company were hurt and wounded, Sir Patrick Gordon of Auchindown, his uncle, a wise, valiant, and resolute knight, with 14 others, were there slain. All their hurt men were carried that night to Auchindown, where most part of them stayed until they were recovered. This battle was fought on Thursday, the 3rd day of October, 1594.

The Lord Forbes, the lairds of Buchan and Drum, assembled all their friends and followers, with intention to join with Argyll; but, hearing of his overthrow, they conclude to join with the Dunbars, and the rest of the forces coming from the provinces of Moray and Ross, and so to invade the Gordons when they came from the battle, thinking it now an easy matter to overthrow them, and to revenge old quarrels. To this effect the whole surname of Forbes, with most part of the Leslies and the Irvines, met at Druminour (the Lord Forbes's dwelling) and so went on, thinking to overtake Argyll, and to cause him return and renew the battle against the Gordons and their partakers; but, as they marched forward, a gentleman called Irvine was killed with the shot of a pistol, in the dark of the night, hard by the Lord Forbes, the author of which shot was never yet known until this day; for presently all their pistols were searched and found to be full. This unexpected accident bred such a confusion and amazement in the minds of the Forbeses and their followers, being now all afraid of one another, that they dissolved their companies, and returned home. The rest of the clans in the north, such as the Dunbars, the Frasers, the Munroes, and the Clan Kenzie, being convened at Forres in Moray, were stayed by the policy of Dunbar of Moyness, who was then tutor to the Sheriff of Moray, and favoured the Earl of Huntly, Sir Patrick Gordon of Auchindown having married his mother.

Whilst the Earl of Argyll was thus employed against Huntly, the King came to Dundee, where he expected the issue of that battle; which, when he had heard, His

Majesty took journey north toward Strathbogie. In this voyage His Majesty, by the instigation of Huntly and Errol's greatest enemies, permitted (though unwillingly) divers houses to be thrown down, such as the house of Strathbogie, which appertained to Huntly, the house of Slaines, in Buchan, appertaining to the Earl of Errol, the house of Culsamond, in Garioch, appertaining to the Laird of Newton Gordon, the house of Bagays, in Angus, appertaining to Sir Walter Lindsay, and the house of Craig, in Angus, appertaining to Sir John Ogilvy, son to the Lord Ogilvy.

In this meantime that the King was at Strathbogie, the Earl of Huntly, with divers of his friends, went into Sutherland and Caithness; and, when His Majesty returned into Edinburgh, Huntly left the Kingdom, and travelled through Germany, France, and Flanders; having stayed abroad one year and five months, he was recalled again by the King; and, at his return, both he, Angus, and Errol were again restored to their former honours and dignities, at a Parliament held in Edinburgh in

November, 1597; and further, His Majesty honoured the Earl of Huntly with the honour of Marquis, the year 1599. All quarrels betwixt him and the Earls of Argyll and Moray were taken away by the marriage of Argyll's eldest daughter, to George, Lord Gordon, Huntly's eldest son, and by the marriage of Lady Anne Gordon, Huntly's daughter, to James, Earl of Moray, son to him that was slain at Dunibristle.

The Troubles betwixt the Forbeses and the Gordons in the Years 1571 and 1572.

The two families of Gordon and Forbes were of great power and authority in their country, both of them valiant, wise, and wealthy; both harbouring deadly feud, long rooted between them. The Gordons then lived with great concord and unity among themselves; and, by the tolerance of their Kings, had, for many years, governed the people adjoining unto them, whereby they became wealthy and of great power, and purchased strength among themselves, together with the attendance and following of other men towards them. When, on the contrary, the Forbeses were at war one with another, they daily impaired their own strength with their own slaughters, and, in end, wrought their own harm by pressing to strive against the Gordons. These two surnames did live together at this time, rather in secret emulation than open envy; because they had (in way of reconciliation) by marriage intermingled their families tegether; but their hid and long-rooted rancour did now burst forth, not only by following contrary factions during these civil wars betwixt the King's party and the Queen's, but chiefly because that John, Master of Forbes (eldest son to the Lord Forbes), had repudiated and put away his wife, Margaret Gordon, daughter to George, Earl of Huntly, which he did by the instigation of his uncle, Black Arthur Forbes, who mortally hated the Gordons. This Arthur was a man of great courage, ambitious, and ready to undertake anything whatsoever for the advancement and reconciliation of his family. The Forbeses, from the first time of these civil discords in

Scotland, did follow the King's party; the Gordons did always remain constantly faithful to the Queen, even unto the end.

The Forbeses, by persuasion of Black Arthur Forbes, had appointed both day and place of meeting, where they should assemble together, not only for their own general reconciliation among themselves, but also to enterprise something against the Gordons and the rest of the Queen's favourers in these parts; whereof Adam Gordon of Achindown having secret intelligence (his brother, the Earl of Huntly, being then in Edinburgh), he assembled a certain number of his kindred and followers to cross the proceedings of the Forbeses, who were all convened at Tillieangus, above Druminour, in the beginning of the year of God 1572. The Forbeses perceiving the Gordons coming up towards them, against the hill where they then were, they did intrench themselves within their camp, which they had strongly fortified, dividing their army into two several companies, whereof Black Arthur Forbes commanded that which lay next unto the Gordons. Adam Gordon (far inferior in number to his enemies), presently, without

The Feuds of the Clans

any stay, fiercely invaded the first company; his brother, Mr. Robert Gordon, set upon the other; so, breaking their trenches, they ran desperately upon the spears of their enemies. After a sharp and cruel conflict, courageously fought a long time on either side, Black Arthur Forbes, with divers others, gentlemen of his surname and family, were slain; the rest were all overthrown, put to flight, and chased even to the gates of Druminour, the Lord Forbes's chief dwelling-place; few of the Gordons were killed, but only John Gordon of Buckie, father to John Gordon of Buckie, now living.

The Forbeses attempted nothing afterward in revenge of this overthrow, until the time that John, Master of Forbes (Black Arthur's nephew and chief of that family), hardly escaping from his enemies, hastened to Court, where the Earl of Mar, then Regent, had his residence, hoping by him to be relieved. The Regent gave him five companies of footmen and some horsemen, with letters to such of the adjoining nobility as favoured and followed that party, desiring them to associate and join themselves unto the Forbeses. These, then, being confederated and assembled together with certain other families of their affinity and neighbours, so advanced the spirit of this John, Master of Forbes, that he now thought himself sufficiently furnished against the forces of his adversaries, and so presently went to Aberdeen, to expel Adam Gordon from thence, the year of God 1572, who, knowing the preparation of the Forbeses, and understanding the approach of the enemies so near at hand, assembled such of his friends and followers as he could soonest find at that time, and led them out of the town. He sent a company of musketeers, under the conduct of Captain Thomas Carr, to a convenient place where the Forbeses must of necessity pass, there to lie in ambush, and not to stir till the battle did join; then he sent certain of the Sutherland bowmen (who had retired themselves out of their country during the Earl of Sutherland's minority), and desired them to draw a great compass about, and so, to set upon the back of the Forbeses' footmen and musketeers; he himself, and his brother, Mr Robert Gordon, with the residue of his company, stayed the coming of the Forbeses at a place called

Craibstane, not far from the ports of the new town of Aberdeen.

The Forbeses, being in sight of Aberdeen, began to consult among themselves what was best to be done; some were of opinion that the fittest and safest course was to go to Old Aberdeen, and there seat themselves, and from thence to molest the new town, and compel Adam Gordon to depart from New Aberdeen, by the aid and assistance of these experienced footmen which were sent from the Regent: but the Master of Forbes and his kinsmen would not hearken thereto, desiring present battle, which was then concluded; and so the Forbeses advanced with great courage against the Gordons, who received them with the like resolution. At the very first encounter, Achindown's musketeers, who lay in ambush, killed a number of the Forbeses; then both the armies joined with great violence. After a cruel conflict, with incredible obstinacy on either side, the Laird of Pitsligo (Forbes's) two brethren, with divers other gentlemen of the surname of Forbes, were there slain; Captain Chisholm, with the footmen (sent by the Regent to their support) were put to flight by the

Sutherland bowmen, who pursued them eagerly with great slaughter. Among the rest, Captain Chisholm was slain, with three other Captains, which the rest of the Forbeses perceiving, they fled apace; many of the principals were taken, with their Chief and General, John, Master of Forbes, whose father was then very aged, lying sick at Druminour, expecting the sorrowful news of this overthrow. Adam Gordon used this victory very moderately, and suffered no man to be killed after the fury of the fight was past. When all was ended, he returned to the Church of Aberdeen, and there gave thanks unto God for his happy success. Alexander Forbes of Strathgarnock (author of all the trouble betwixt these two families, and the chief stirrer-up of Arthur Forbes against the Gordons) was taken at this battle, and, as they were going to behead him, Achindown caused them to stay his execution. He entertained the Master of Forbes, and the rest of the prisoners, with great kindness and courtesy; he carried the Master of Forbes along with him to Strathbogie; and in the end gave him and all the rest leave to depart.

The next ensuing summer after this conflict

at Craibstane, Adam Gordon of Achindown, following his victory, entered the Mearns, and besieged the house of Glenbervie, putting all the Regent's party within that province into a great fear and tumult.

The Earl of Crawford, the Lords Grey, Ogilvy, and Glamis, taking part with the Regent against the Queen, assembled all the forces of Angus and Mearns to resist Achindown, and to stop his passage at Brechin, where they encamped; but Adam Gordon, being advertised of their proceedings, left the most part of his men at the siege of Glenbervie, from whence he parted in the dead time of the night, with the most resolute men of his company, to invade these lords; and being come to Brechin, he killed the watch with divers others, surprised the town, set upon the lords, chased them, and made himself master of the town and castle of Brechin.

The next morning, the lords understanding Achindown's small forces in regard of theirs, they assembled their men together, and came near unto Brechin to fight against him, who met them with resolute courage; but as they were ready to encounter, the lords, not able to endure the first charge of their enemies, fled apace with all their companies. There were slain of them above 80; and divers of them were taken, amongst whom was the Lord Glamis, who was carried to Strathbogie, and, being detained there a while, he was set at liberty with the rest. This conflict was called the Bourd of Brechin.

Then returned Adam Gordon back again to the siege of Glenbervie, and took it; from thence he went to Montrose, and took that town. In his return from thence, he took the Castle of Dun, which appertained to the Regent's cousin, and so marched forward into Angus. The inhabitants of Dundee hearing of his approach, and despairing of their own abilities to resist him, they sent for help into Fife; but Achindown, having done his pleasure in Angus and Mearns, returned home into the North, being contented for that time with what he had already done against his enemies. By this good success of the Gordons, the Queen's favourers in all the parts of the kingdom were highly encouraged at that time.

THE BRIG OF DEE.

The year of God 1588, there were some secret emulations and factions at Court. The Earl of Huntly being in favour with His Majesty, obtained the Captaincy of His Majesty's Guards, which the Master of Glamis had before; for this cause the Master of Glamis and his associates, joining themselves to the English Ambassador, then lying at Edinburgh, do surmise to the King's Majesty, that some letters of the Earl of Huntly's, sent by him to the King of Spain, were intercepted in England. Huntly was called to make his answer; he compears, and denies these letters to have been written or sent by him, but only devised by his enemies, thereby to put him in disgrace with his master; yet he is warded in the Castle of Edinburgh in the latter end of February, and being tried, he is released the 7th day of March following; whereupon the Earls of Huntly, Crawford, and Errol, address themselves into the North, and take journey towards St. Johnstown, where they were advertised that the Earls

of Athol and Morton and the Master of
Glamis had convened forces to entrap them
within St. Johnstown. Huntly, Errol, and
Crawford issued forth of that town, with
such small companies as they then had, and
rencountered with the Master of Glamis,
whom they chased and apprehended in Kirkhill,
and carried him prisoner with them into the
North.

Chancellor Maitland and the rest of the
Master of Glamis's faction at Court, hearing
of this accident, they inflame the King with
anger against Huntly and his associates, and
do persuade His Majesty to take a journey
into the North. Huntly, in the meantime,
assembles all his friends and dependants, to
the number of 10,000 men, and came forward
to the Brig of Dee, with a resolution to fight
against his enemies, the 20th of April, the
year 1589; but being certainly informed that
the King was coming in person against him,
he dissolved his army, and submitted himself
to His Majesty, withal releasing the Master
of Glamis from captivity; whereupon Huntly
was committed to ward at Edinburgh, then
at Borthwick, thereafter at Finnerin; from

whence he was shortly afterward released by His Majesty. The Earl of Errol was also warded in Edinburgh Castle, where he was detained until he paid a sum of money, which was employed to the use of Chancellor Maitland.

A TUMULT IN ROSS IN 1597.

The year of God 1597, there happened an accident in Ross, at a fair in Lagavraid, which had almost put Ross and all the neighbouring counties in a combustion. The quarrel did begin betwixt John Macgillichallum (brother to the Laird of Raasay), and Alexander Bane (brother to Duncan Bane of Tulloch). The Munroes did assist Alexander Bane, and the Clan Kenzie took part with John Macgillichallum, who was there slain, with John Mac-Murdo Mac-William, and three others of the Clan Kenzie. Alexander Bane escaped, but there were killed on his side John Munro of Culcraggie, with his brother, Hutcheon Munro, and John Munro Robertson. Hereupon the Clan Kenzie and the Munroes began to employ the aid and assistance of their friends

132   *The Feuds of the Clans*

from all parts to invade one another; but they were in some measure reconciled by the mediation of indifferent friends and neighbours.

THE DEATH OF SIR LAUCHLAN MACLEAN IN 1598.

Sir Lauchlan Maclean's ambition, together with his desire of revenge, thrust him on to claim the inheritance of the whole Isle of Isla, being always the possession and ancient inheritance of the Clan Donald, all which Maclean thought easily now to compass, Sir James Macdonald (the just inheritor thereof) being young, and his father, Angus Macdonald, aged. Sir Lauchlan assembled his whole forces, and, in warlike manner, invaded Isla, to take possession thereof by virtue of a new right which he had then lately obtained, which Sir James Macdonald (Maclean's sister's son) understanding, he convened his friends, and went likewise into the same island (being his own and his forebears' possession) to interrupt, if it were possible, the proceedings of his unkind uncle, Maclean.

Being both arrived in the island, such as did love them and desired peace, did mediate a long time betwixt them, and took great pains in essaying to agree them. Sir James (being the more reasonable of the two) was content to let his uncle have the half of the island during his lifetime, although he had no just title thereto, providing he would take it in the same fashion as his predecessors, the Clan Lean, had it even before his time, to wit, holden of the Clan Donald; and, moreover, he offered to submit the controversy to the King's Majesty's arbitrament, thereby to eschrew all debate with his uncle. But Maclean, running headlong to his own mischief, much against the opinion of his friends, who advised him to the contrary, did refuse all offers of peace, unless his nephew would then presently resign unto him the title and possession of the whole island. Whereupon they do both resolve and prepare to fight, Sir James being far inferior in number of men, but some of these he had with him were lately before trained in the wars of Ireland. Thus there ensued a cruel and sharp battle, at the head of Loch-

134   The Feuds of the Clans

Gruinart, in Isla, courageously fought a long time on either side. Sir James, in the beginning, caused his vanguard to make a compass in fashion of a retreat, thereby to get the sun at his back, and the advantage of a hill which was hard by. In the end, Sir James, having repulsed the enemy's vanguard, and forcing their main battle, Maclean was slain, courageously fighting, together with 80 of the most principal men of his kin, and 200 common soldiers lying dead about him. His son, Lauchlan Barrach Maclean (being sore wounded) was chased with the rest of his men even to their boats and vessels. Sir James Macdonald was dangerously wounded, whereof he hardly recovered afterward, for he was shot with an arrow through the body, and was left the most part of the ensuing night for dead amongst the slain bodies. There were slain of the Clan Donald about 30 in all, and above 60 wounded, which happened the year of God 1598.

And thus the war began by Maclean, without reason, the year of God 1585, ended now, this year, by his death. Maclean had three responses from a witch before he undertook this journey into Isla; first, desiring him not to land there upon Thursday; the next was, forbidding him to drink of a well beside Gruinart; and thirdly, she told him that one called Maclean should be slain at Gruinart. The first he transgressed unwillingly, being driven into that island by a tempest on a Thursday. The second he transgressed negligently, and drank of that water before he knew the name of the place, and so he died at Gruinart, as was foretold him, but doubtfully, and as commonly all such responses be. These broils and uproars did so move the King against the Macdonalds, that His Majesty afterwards finding the inheritance both of Kintyre and Isla to beat his own disposition, he gave all these lands to the Earl of Argyle and the Campbells; whereupon proceeded the troubles that arose since betwixt the Campbells and the Clan Donald in Kintyre and Isla, after His Majesty's coming to the Crown of England, which I omit to relate; only thus far, that Sir James Macdonald was, by Argyle's means, warded in the Castle of Edinburgh, and was kept there a long time; from whence he escaped by the means and diligence of his cousin, MacRanald, who fled with Sir James into Spain and Flanders, where they were entertained by the Spaniards; from whence they are now (upon the Earl of Argyle's flight thither to the King of Spain) both recalled home by His Majesty, the year of God 1620, and are now in England at this time, with the King, who hath given Sir James a yearly pension of 1000 merks sterling, and a yearly pension of 200 merks sterling to MacRanald, together with a pardon for all their bye-gone offences.

TROUBLES IN THE WEST ISLES BETWIXT THE CLAN DONALD AND THE SIOL TORMOIT IN 1601.

Donald Gorm Macdonald of the Sleat had married Sir Rory Macleod of the Harris's sister, and for some displeasure or jealousy conceived against her, he did repudiate her; whereupon Sir Rory Macleod sent a message to Donald Gorm, desiring him to take home his sister. Donald Gorm not only refused

The Feuds of the Clans

to obey his request, but also intended divorcement against her; which when he had obtained, he married Kenneth Mackenzie, Lord of Kintail's sister.

Sir Rory Macleod took this disgrace (as he thought it) so highly, that, assembling his countrymen and followers without delay, he invaded, with fire and sword, a part of Donald Gorm's lands in the Isle of Skye, which lands Sir Rory claimed to appertain to himself. Donald Gorm, impatient of this injury, convened his forces, and went into the Harris, which he wasted and spoiled, carried away their store and bestial, and killed some of the inhabitants. This again did so stir up Sir Rory Macleod and his kin, the Siol Tormoit, that they took a journey into the Isle of Uist (which appertaineth to Donald Gorm), and landing there, Sir Rory sent his cousin, Donald Glas Macleod, with some 40 men, to spoil the island, and to take a prey of goods out of the precinct of Kiltrynaid, where the people had put all their goods to be preserved as in a sanctuary, being a church. John Macian-MacJames (a kinsman of Donald Gorm's) being desired by him to stay in the island, accompanied with 20 others, rencountered with Donald Glas Macleod. This small company of the Clan Donald behaved themselves so valiantly, that, after a sharp skirmish, they killed Donald Glas Macleod, with the most part of his company, and so rescued the goods. Sir Rory, seeing the bad success of his kinsmen, retired home for that time.

Thus both parties were bent headlong against others with a spirit full of revenge and fury, and so continued mutually infesting one another with spoils and cruel slaughters, to the utter ruin and desolation of both countries, until the inhabitants were forced to eat horses, dogs, cats, and other filthy beasts. In end, Donald Gorm assembled his whole forces the year of God 1601, to try the event of battle, and came to invade Sir Rory's lands, thinking thereby to draw his enemies to fight. Sir Rory Macleod was then in Argyle, craving aid and advice from the Earl of Argyle against the Clan Donald. Alexander Macleod (Sir Rory's brother) resolves to fight with Donald Gorm, though his brother was absent; so, assembling all the inhabitants of his brother's lands, with the whole race of the Siol Tormoit, and some of the Siol Torquil, out of the Lewis, he encamped beside a hill called Ben-a-Chuilinn, in the Isle of Skye, with a resolution to fight against Donald Gorm and the Clan Donald the next morning, which were no sooner come but there ensued a cruel and terrible skirmish, which lasted the most part of the day, both contending for the victory with great obstinacy. The Clan Donald, in the end, overthrew their enemies, hurt Alexander Macleod, and took him prisoner, with Neil MacAlister Roy, and 30 others of the chiefest men among the Siol Tormoit, killed two near kinsmen of Sir Rory Macleod's, John MacTormoit and Tormot MacTormoit, with many others. After this skirmish there followed a reconciliation betwixt them, by the mediation of old Angus Macdonald of Kintyre, the Laird of Coll, and others. Then Donald Gorm delivered unto Sir Rory Macleod all the prisoners taken at Ben-a-Chuilinn, together with his brother, Alexander Macleod; since which time they have continued in peace and quietness.

The Troubles between Lord Kintail and Glengarry.

The year of God 1602, the Lord Kintail, and his kin the Clan Kenzie, fell at variance with the Laird of Glengarry (one of the Clan Donald), who, being unexpert and unskilful in the laws of the realms, the Clan Kenzie intrapped and insnared him within the compass thereof, and charged him, with a number of his men and followers, to compear before the Justice at Edinburgh, they having, in the meantime, slain two of his kinsmen. Glengarry, not knowing or neglecting the charges, came not to Edinburgh at the prefixed day, but went about, at his own hand, to revenge the slaughter of his kinsmen. Thereupon, the Lord of Kintail, by his credit in Council, doth purchase a commission against Glengarry and his countrymen; which, being obtained, Kintail (with the assistance of the next adjoining neighbours, by virtue of his Commission) went into Morar (which appertained to Glengarry), and wasted all that country; then, in his return from Morar, he besieged the Castle of Strome, which, in the end, he took, by treason of the Captain unto whom Glengarry had committed the custody thereof. Afterward, the Clan Kenzie did invade Glengarry's eldest son, whom they killed with forty of his followers, not without some slaughter of the Clan Kenzie likewise. In end, after great slaughter on either side, they came to an agreement, wherein Glengarry (for to obtain his peace) was glad to requite and renounce to the Lord of Kintail, the perpetual inheritance of the Strome, with the lands adjacent.

Troubles in the Island of Raasay in 1611.

In the month of August, 1611, there happened an accident in the Isle of Raasay, which is among the West Isles, where GilleCallum, Laird of Raasay, and Murdoch Mackenzie (son to the Laird of Gairloch), with some others, were slain, upon this occasion. The lands of Gairloch did sometime pertain to the Lairds of Raasay, his predecessors, and when the surname of Clan Kenzie began first to rise and to flourish, one of them did obtain the third part of Gairloch in wadset; and thus once getting footing therein, shortly thereafter, doth purchase a pretended right to the whole, which the lawful inheritors did neglect; whereby, in process of time, the Clan Kenzie do challenge the whole, whereof the Laird of Gairloch, his father, obtains the possession, excluding the Laird of Raasay and his kin, the Clan Vic-GilleChallum, whom Gairloch and the Clan Kenzie did pursue with fire and sword, and chased them out of Gairloch. In like manner, the Clan Vic-GilleChallum invaded the Laird of Gairloch and his country with spoils and slaughters. In end, the Laird of Gairloch apprehended John MacAllan, and chased John Tolmach, two principal men of the race of Clan Vic-GilleChallum, and near cousins to the Laird of Raasay, at which skirmish there was slaughter on either side, the year of God 1610. The Laird of Gairloch, not fully satisfied herewith, he sent his son Murdoch, accompanied with Alexander Bane (son and heir to Alexander Bane of Tulloch), and some others, to search and pursue John Tolmach; and to this effect he did hire a ship (which then, by chance, happened to lie upon that coast) to transport his son Murdoch, with his company, into the Isle of Skye, where he understood John Tolmach to be at that time. But how soon Murdoch, with his company, were embarked, they turned their course another way, and (whether of set purpose, or constrained thereto by contrary winds, I know not) arrived at the Isle of Raasay, running headlong to their own destruction. The Laird of Raasay, perceiving the ship in the harbour, went aboard to buy some wines and other commodities, accompanied with twelve men. How soon Murdoch did see them coming, he, with all his company (lest they should be known or seen), went to the lower rooms of the ship, until the other party had gone away. The Laird of Raasay entered the ship, and, having spoken the mariner, he departed with a resolution to return quickly. Murdoch, understanding that they were gone, came out of the lower rooms, and perceiving them come again, he resolved not to conceal himself any longer. The Laird of Raasay desired his brother, Murdoch MacGilleChallum, to follow him into the ship with more company, in another galley, that they might carry to the shore some wine and other provisions which he had resolved to buy from the mariner; so the Laird of Raasay, returning to the ship, and finding Gairloch's son there, beyond his expectations, he adviseth with his men, and thereupon resolveth to take him prisoner, in pledge of his cousin, John MacAllan, whom Gairloch detained in captivity. They began first to quarrel, then to fight in the ship, which continued all day long. In the end, the Laird of Raasay was slain, and divers of his men; so was Murdoch, the son of Gairloch, and Alexander Bane killed, with their whole company, three only excepted, who fought so manfully that they killed all those that came into the ship with the Laird of Raasay, and hurt a number of those that were with Murdoch MacGilleChallum in two galleys hotly pursuing them. At last, feeling deadly hurt, and not able to endure any longer, they sailed away with prosperous wind, and died shortly thereafter.

The Troubles of the Lewis.

Rory Macleod of the Lewis had three wives; he married, first, Barbara Stewart, daughter to the Lord Methven, by whom he had Torquil Oighre, who died before his father, without issue. After Barbara Stewart's death, Rory married Mackenzie's daughter, who bore Torquil Connaldagh, whom Rory would not acknowledge as his son, but held him always a bastard; and, repudiating his mother, he married Maclean's sister, by whom he had Torquil Dow and Tormot. Besides these, Rory had three base sons—Neil Macleod, Rory Oig, and Murdo Macleod. After the death of old Rory Macleod, his son, Torquil Dow Macleod (excluding his brother Torquil Connaldagh as a bastard), doth take possession of the Lewis, and is acknowledged by the inhabitants as the lawful inheritor of that Island. Torquil Connaldagh (by some called Torquil of the Oogaidh) perceiving himself thus put bye the inheritance of the Lewis, hath recourse to his mother's kindred, the Clan Mackenzie, and desires their support to recover the same.

The Lord Kintail, Torquil Connaldagh, his brother—Murdo Macleod, and the Brieve of the Lewis, met altogether in Ross, to advise by what means Torquil Connaldagh might obtain the possession of the Lewis, which they were out of all hope to effect so long as Torquil Dow was alive; whereupon the Brieve of the Lewis undertook to slay his master, Torquil Dow, which he brings thus to pass:—The Brieve, being accompanied with the most part of his tribe (the Clan-vic-Gill-Mhoire), went in his galley to the Isle of Rona; and, by the way, he apprehended a Dutch ship, which he brought by force along with him to the Lewis; he invites his master, Torquil Dow, to a banquet in the ship; Torquil Dow (suspecting no deceit) went thither, accompanied with seven of the best of his friends, and sat down in the ship, expecting some drink; instead of wine, they bring cords; thus were they all apprehended and bound by the Brieve and his kindred, who brought them to the Lord of Kintail's bounds, and there beheaded them every man, in July, 1597. Neither did this advance Torquil Connaldagh to the possession of the Lewis; for his brother,

The Feuds of the Clans

Neil Macleod, opposed himself, and pursued the Brieve and his kin in a part of the Island called Ness, which they had fortified, where he killed divers of them, and made them leave the strength. Thus did Neil Macleod possess the Island, to the behoof of his brother, Tormot, and the children of Torquil Dow, whom he acknowledged to be righteous heirs of the Island. Torquil Connaldagh had now lost both his sons, John and Neil, and had married his daughter to Rory Mackenzie (the Lord Kintail's brother), giving her in marriage the lands of Ooigeach. Hereupon, Kintail began to think and advise by what means he might purchase to himself the inheritance of that Island, having now Torquil Connaldagh and his brother, Murdo Macleod, altogether at his devotion, and having Tormot Macleod in his custody, whom he took from the schools; so that he had no one to oppose his designs but Neil Macleod, whom he might easily overthrow. Kintail deals earnestly with Torquil Connaldagh, and, in end, persuades him to resign the right of the Island into his favour, and to deliver him all the old rights and evidents of the Lewis.

In this meantime, the barons and gentlemen of Fife, hearing these troubles, were enticed, by the persuasion of some that had been there, and by the report of the fertility of the Island, to undertake a difficult and hard enterprise. They conclude to send a colony thither, and to civilise (if it were possible) the inhabitants of the Island. To this effect, they obtain, from the King, a gift of the Lewis, the year 1599, or thereabouts, which was alleged to be then at his disposal. Thereupon, the adventurers, being joined together in Fife, assembled a company of soldiers, with artificers of all sorts, and did transport them into the Lewis, where they erected houses and buildings, till, in end, they made a pretty little town, in a proper and convenient place fit for the purpose, and there they encamped themselves. Neil Macleod and Murdo (the sons of old Rory) withstood the undertakers. Murdo Macleod invaded the Laird of Barcolmy, whom he apprehended, together with his ship, and killed all his men; so, having detained him six months in captivity in the Lewis, he released him from his promise to pay him a ransom.

The Feuds of the Clans 149

Now, Neil Macleod was grieved in heart to see his brother, Murdo, entertain the Brieve and his tribe, being the chief instruments of their brother, Torquil Dow's, slaughter; and, thereupon, Neil apprehended his brother, Murdo, which, when the undertakers heard, they sent a message to Neil, showing that, if he would deliver unto them his brother Murdo, they would agree with himself, give him a portion of the Island, and assist him to revenge the slaughter of his brother, Torquil Dow. Whereunto Neil hearkened, delivered his brother, Murdo, to the undertakers; then went Neil with them to Edinburgh, and had his pardon from the King for all his by-past offences. Murdo Macleod was executed at St. Andrews.

Thus was the Earl of Kintail in despair to purchase or obtain the Lewis; and therefore he lends all his wits to cross the undertakers; he setteth Tormot Macleod at liberty, thinking that, at his arrival in the Island, all the inhabitants would stir in his favour against the undertakers; which they did indeed, as the natural inclination is of all these Islanders and Highlanders, who, of all other people, are most bent and willing to hazard and adventure themselves, their lives, and all they have, for their lords and masters. The King was informed, by the undertakers, that the Lord of Kintail was a crosser and a hinderer of their enterprise; whereupon he was brought into question, and committed to ward in the Castle of Edinburgh, from whence he was released, without the trial of an assize, by the Lord Chancellor's means. Neil Macleod, returning into the Lewis with the undertakers, fell at variance with them; whereupon, he went about to invade their camp, and they began, in like manner, to lay a snare for him. The Laird of Wormistoun, choosing a very dark night, sent a company to apprehend Neil; who, perceiving them coming, invaded them, and chased them, with slaughter, to their camp. By this time, came Tormot Macleod into the Island, at whose arrival the inhabitants speedily assembled, and came to him as to their lord and master.

Thereupon, Tormot, accompanied with his brother, Neil, invaded the camp of the undertakers, forced it, burnt the fort, killed most part of their men, took their commanders prisoners, and released them after eight months' captivity. Thus, for a while, Tormot Macleod commanded in that Island, until the undertakers returned again to the Lewis, being assisted by the forces of all the neighbouring countries, by virtue of the King's commission, directed against Tormot Macleod and his kin, the Siol-Torquil. How soon their forces were landed on the Island, Tormot Macleod rendered himself to the undertakers, upon their promise to carry him safe to London, and to obtain him a remission for his byepast crimes; but Neil Macleod stood out and would not submit himself. Tormot being come to London, the King gives him a pardon; but, withal, he sent him home into Scotland, to be kept in ward at Edinburgh, where he remained until the month of March, 1615, that the King gave him liberty to pass into Holland, where he ended his days. Tormot thus warded in Edinburgh, the adventurers did settle themselves again for a little while, in the Lewis, where, at last, the undertakers began to weary; many of the adventurers and partners drew back from the enterprise; some, for lack of means, were not able;

others died; others had greater occasion and business elsewhere to abstract them; many of them began to decline and decay in their estates; and so, being continually vexed by Neil Macleod, they left the Island, and returned into Fife.

The Lord of Kintail, perceiving all things thus fall out to his mind, did now show himself openly in the matter. He passed a gift of the Island in his own name, under His Majesty's great seal, by the Lord Chancellor's means, by virtue of the old right which Torquil Connaldagh had before resigned in his favour. Some of the adventurers complained hereof to the King's Majesty, who was highly displeased with Kintail, and made him resign his right into His Majesty's hands; which right, being now at His Majesty's disposition, he gave the same to three of the undertakers, to wit, the Lord Balmerino, Sir James Spence of Wormistoun, and Sir George Hay; who, now having all the right in their persons, assembled their forces together, with the aid of most part of all the neighbouring counties; and so, under the conduct of Sir George Hay and Sir James Spence, they invaded the Lewis again, not only to settle a colony there, but also to search for Neil Macleod.

The Lord Kintail (yet hunting after the Lewis) did, underhand, assist Neil, and publicly did aid the undertakers by virtue of the King's commission; Kintail sent a supply of victuals, in a ship from Ross, to the adventurers. In the meantime, he sent quietly to Neil Macleod, desiring him to take the ship by the way, that the undertakers, trusting to these victuals, and being disappointed thereof, might be forced to return, and abandon the Island; which fell out accordingly; for Sir James Spence and Sir George Hay, failing to apprehend Neil, and being scarce of victuals to furnish their army, began to weary, and so dismissed all the neighbouring forces. Sir George Hay and Wormistoun then retired into Fife, leaving some men in the Island to defend and keep the fort until they sent them a fresh supply of men and victuals; whereupon, Neil, being assisted by his nephew, Malcolm Macleod (the son of Rory Og), invaded the undertakers' camp, burnt the same, apprehended all those which were left behind in the island, and sent them home safely; since which time they never returned again into the Lewis. Then did the Lord Balmerino, Sir George Hay, and Sir James Spence, begin to weary of the Lewis, and sold their title of that Island to the Lord of Kintail for a sum of money; whereby, in end, after great trouble and much blood, he obtained that Island. And thus did this enterprise of the Fife undertakers come to no effect, after they had spent much time, and most part of their means, about it.

Kintail was glad that he had now, at last, caught his long-expected prey; and thereupon he went into the Island, where he was no sooner landed but all the inhabitants yielded unto him, except Neil Macleod, and some few others. The inhabitants yielded the more willingly to Kintail because he was their neighbour, and might still vex them with continual excursions if they did stand out against him; which they were not able to do. Neil Macleod was now forced to retire to a rock, within the sea, called Berrissay, which he kept for the space of three years. During the time of his stay in the fort of Berrissay, there arrived an English pirate in the Lewis, who had a ship furnished with great wealth;

this pirate (called Peter Lowe) entered into friendship and familiarity with Neil, being both rebels; at last, Neil took him prisoner with all his men, whom he sent, together with the ship, to the Council of Scotland, thinking thereby to get his own pardon, and his brother Tormot released out of prison; but neither of them did he obtain; and all the Englishmen, with their captain, Peter Lowe, were hanged at Leith, the year 1612. Neil Macleod, being wearied to remain in the fort of Berrissay, abandoned the same, and, dispersing all his company several ways, he retired into Harris, where he remained a certain while in secret; then he rendered himself unto his cousin, Sir Rory Macleod, whom he entreated to carry him into England to His Majesty; which Sir Rory undertook to do; and, coming to Glasgow, with a resolution to embark then for England, he was charged there, under the pain of treason, to deliver Neil, whom he presented before the Council at Edinburgh, where he was executed in April, 1613. After the death of Neil, his nephew, Malcolm Macleod (the son of Rory Og), escaping from the Tutor of Kintail, associated himself to the Clan Donald, in Isla and Kintyre, during their troubles against the Campbells, in the years 1614, 1615, and 1616; at which time Malcolm made a journey from Kintyre to the Lewis, and there killed two gentlemen of the Clan Mackenzie; then he went into Spain, and there remained in Sir James Macdonald's company, with whom he is now again returned into England, in the year 1620.

SOME TROUBLES BETWIXT SUTHERLAND AND CAITHNESS IN 1612.

The year of God 1612, there happened some discord and dissensions betwixt Sutherland and Caithness, which troubled a little the peace of that part of the kingdom. The occasion was this:—One Arthur Smith (a false coiner), being, together with his servant, apprehended for making and striking of false money, were both sent to Edinburgh, the year of God 1599, where his servant was executed, but Arthur himself escaped, and retired into Caithness, and dwelt there with the Earl of that country. The report hereof coming to the King's ears, the year of God 1612, His Majesty gave a secret commission to his servant, Sir Robert Gordon (the Earl of Sutherland's brother), for apprehending this Arthur Smith; but, as Sir Robert was going about to perform the same, he received a commandment from His Majesty to accompany Sir Alexander Hay (then Secretary of Scotland) in apprehending John Lesley of New Lesley, and some other rebels in Gereagh; which Sir Robert obeyed, and committed the execution of the commission against Arthur Smith unto his nephew, Donald Mackay of Farr, John Gordon of Gospeter, younger (nephew to George Gordon slain at Marle, the year 1587), and to John Gordon, son to John Gordon of Backies. These three, parting from Sutherland with 36 men, came to the town of Thurso in Caithness, where Arthur Smith then dwelt, and there apprehended him; which, when John Sinclair of Skirkag (the Earl of Caithness's nephew) understood, he assembled the inhabitants of the town, and opposed himself to the King's commission. There ensued a sharp skirmish upon the streets of Thurso, where John Sinclair of Skirkag was slain, and James Sinclair of Dun left there, deadly hurt, lying upon the ground; Arthur Smith was there likewise slain; divers of the Sutherland men were hurt; but, perceiving Smith dead, they left Thurso, and retired themselves all home into their own country.

Thereupon, both the parties compeared before the Secret Council at Edinburgh. The Earl of Caithness did pursue Sir Robert Gordon, Donald Mackay, and John Gordon, for the slaughter of his nephew. These, again, did pursue the inhabitants of Caithness for resisting the King's commissioners. The Secret Council (having special commandment from His Majesty to that effect) dealt earnestly with both the parties; and, in end, persuaded them to submit these questions and debates to the arbitrament of friends. A certain number of the Lords of Council were chosen as friends for either party. The Archbishop of St. Andrews and the Earl of Dunfermline, Chancellor of Scotland, were appointed oversmen by consent of both the parties. These friendly judges, having heard the business reasoned in their presence, and, finding that the examination thereof would prove tedious

and intricate, they direct a power to the
Marquis of Huntly to deal in the matter;
desiring him to try, if, by his means and
mediation, these contentions might be settled,
happening betwixt parties so strictly tied to
him by blood and alliance, the Earl of Sutherland being his cousin-german, and the Earl
of Caithness having married his sister. The
Marquis of Huntly did his best, but could not
prevail, either party being so far from condescending to the other's demands, and so he
remitted the business back again to the
Secret Council; which Sir Robert Gordon
perceiving, he moved the King's Majesty for
a pardon to Donald Mackay, John Gordon,
and their associates, for the slaughter of
John Sinclair of Skirkag; which His Majesty
earnestly granted, seeing it was committed
in the execution of His Majesty's service;
yet, nevertheless, there still remained a grudge
in the minds of the parties, searching by all
means and occasions to infest one another,
until the year of God 1619, that the Earl of
Caithness and Sir Robert Gordon (then, by his
brother's death, Tutor of Sutherland) were
reconciled by the mediation of George Lord

Gordon, Earl of Enzie, by whose travel and diligence all particulars betwixt the Houses of Sutherland and Caithness were finally settled; and then went both of them familiarly to either's houses; whose perfect reconciliation will, doubtless, tend to the peace and quiet of these parts of the kingdom.

THE SPANISH BLANKS, AND WHAT FOLLOWS THEREUPON.

The year 1592, the Ministry and Church of Scotland thought it necessary that all such as professed the Roman religion in the kingdom should either be compelled to embrace the reformed religion, or else that the censure of excommunication should be used against them, and their goods decerned to appertain to the King so long as they remained disobedient. Mr. George Carr, doctor of laws, was the first that withstood, and was excommunicated; the next was David Graham of Fintrie. This Mr George Carr, considering that hereby he could have no quiet residence within his native country, did deliberate with himself to pass beyond sea into Spain; and, therefore, that he might be the more welcome there, he devised certain blanks, as if they had been subscribed by some of the Scottish nobility, and directed from them to the King of Spain, to be filled up at his pleasure; which project was first hatched by the Jesuits, and chiefly by Father Crightoun, who, for some discontentment, had, a few years before, left Scotland and fled into Spain, where he endeavoured to insinuate himself with King Philip's favour, and published a book concerning the genealogy of his daughter, the Infante, married to the Archduke; wherein he did his best to prove that the two Crowns of England and Scotland did appertain unto her; and, that this cunning Jesuit might the rather move King Philip to make war against the King of Scotland, he wrote books and pamphlets in the disgrace of his own native Prince. Then he adviseth with himself that his next and readiest way was to solicit some of his friends in Scotland, who were of his faith; and, to this effect, he wrote letters, this year, 1592, to this George Carr, and to such of his own colleagues, the Jesuits, as were then in this kingdom, whereby he made them understand what great favour and credit he had with the King of Spain, who, by his persuasions, was resolved both to invade England, and to establish the Catholic faith in Scotland; but, first, that King Philip would be assured of the good-will of the Catholics of Scotland; wherefore he behoved to have certain blanks subscribed by the Catholics, and that he should cause them to be filled up afterwards; which, if he did obtain, he had promise of the King of Spain to send them 250,000 crowns to be distributed among them. After this advertisement of Father Crightoun's, this George Carr (by the advice of the Jesuits then resident in Scotland) devised these blanks, to the effect that George Carr might transport them into Spain. Carr addressed himself to the town of Ayr to have taken shipping there, and, lying in the Isle of Cumrye, attending a fair wind, he was discovered, by the indiscretion of Father Abercromby, and apprehended in the ship; from whence he was carried back to Ayr, and from thence conveyed to Edinburgh. With him was found a packet of letters, directed (as it were) from some Scottish noblemen into Spain and some parts of France; therein were found

blanks alleged subscribed by the Earl of
Angus, the Earl of Huntly, the Earl of Erroll,
and Sir Patrick Gordon of Achindoun, uncle
to the Earl of Huntly. The blanks were
thus, Imprimis, two missive bills directed to
the King of Spain; the one subscribed *de
votre Majesté tres humble et tres obeissant
serviteur, François Comte d'Errol*; another
on this manner, *de votre Majesté tres humble
et tres obeissant serviteur, Guillaume Comte
d'Angus*; item, another blank subscribed by
them all four, as it were by form of con-
tract or obligation conjointly, thus—*Gulielmus
Angusiae Comes, Georgius Comes de Huntley,
Franciscus Erroliae Comes, Patricius Gordon
de Achindowne Miles;* item, a blank subscribed apart by *Franciscus Erroliae Comes;*
item, one by *Georgius Comes de Huntley;*
item, one by *Gulielmus Angusiae Comes.*
Hereupon the Ministers sent some of the
Privy Council to the King to Alloway (where
His Majesty then lay) to advertise him of
these blanks. The King came to Edinburgh,
where all the matter was debated to him at
length, partly by Mr. Bowes Leiger, Ambassador for the Queen of England in Scotland,

and partly by Mr. Robert Bruce, Principal Minister at Edinburgh, showing that the realm of Scotland was in apparent danger of Spaniards to be brought in, by the forenamed earls being Papists; and, thereby, both His Majesty's crown was in danger and the Established religion in hazard to be altered. That Mr. George Carr had sufficiently declared the whole circumstances of the business in his confession, accusing the Popish lords as guilty of these blanks; and thus, taking the matter already *pro confesso*, they urge the business vehemently, and do entreat His Majesty to proceed against them with all celerity and rigour. Then was David Graham of Fintrie apprehended, arraigned, and executed at Edinburgh, in February this year, 1592 (or 1593 *stilo novo*), who, thinking to save himself thereby, did write a long letter, subscribed with his own hand, directed to the King, wherein he made mention that the Roman Catholics of Scotland had undertaken to receive such a number of soldiers as the King of Spain and his Council should appoint; and, in case he would bestow any money for levying of men here, they should willingly both con-

The Feuds of the Clans 165

vey the King's army into England, and retain a certain number in Scotland, for reformation of religion, and to purchase liberty of conscience; that he himself had given counsel thereunto divers times, after that the matter was communicated to him by the Jesuits, and because he fore-knew this purpose, and concealed the same, he was in danger of the law; for this cause, he desired not to be tried by a jury, but offered himself unto the King's mercy and will, when he was arraigned at the bar. The King (not the less of this his voluntary confession) commanded to proceed against him according to the law; which was done.

After this, the King's Majesty (believing certainly that these blanks, together with the informations and intelligence of Father Crightoun concerning the Spanish King, were true indeed) addressed himself to the North of Scotland, for prosecuting Huntly, Angus, and Erroll, and made His Majesty's residence at Aberdeen. Themselves and their dependers were, by open proclamation, at their dwelling-places, required to show their obedience and appearance before the King; but they having understood before the King's coming, and how

His Majesty was incensed and stirred up against them, they had all left their ordinary habitations void. The Countesses of Huntly and Erroll came to the King, to whom he granted their houses and rents, without making any account thereof to His Majesty's Treasurer for the supposed transgression of their husbands.

In this meantime, the Queen of England sent an extraordinary Ambassador into Scotland, whom the King received at Edinburgh, after His Majesty's return from Aberdeen. This Ambassador required that the peace and confederacy concluded and confirmed at Leith, after the expulsing of the French army from Scotland, should now, *de novo*, be ratified by His Majesty in his perfect age; and further, that he should without delay punish the lords and gentlemen suspected of treason, and tried by their own writs and messages; that he should grant them no favour, but extreme rigour; for fear of the inconvenience that should follow upon their wicked pretences, if they were unpunished, when both time and occasion permitted the same. Still the English Ambassador and the Scottish ministers urged the King to call the Catholic lords to a trial of their peers; but the King procured to the ministers this much for them, that, by their favours, they might be brought to be tried without warding; and thereafter to make such satisfaction as should be thought requisite; that in case they were found culpable, to be punished as justice should require; and, if it were otherwise, that they should be absolved; but the ministers would not yield unto the King's pleasure therein, nor permit that the Popish lords should have any trial, till they should be first warded until the nobles should convene to try them. The King refused to ward them until they were found guilty; knowing, by this time, their innocence; for George Carr had refused what he had before, through fear, confessed against the lords, touching the Spanish Blanks. His Majesty was earnest with the ministers that no excommunication should pass against the lords before their trial; which was refused: whereupon there was a Convention of the Estates holden by his Majesty at St. Johnstoun, the year 1593, to curb the power of the presbyterial ministers. There it was resolved (to suppress their liberty) the estate of bishops should be erected and restored. Within a few days after, the King went from St. Johnstoun to the Abbey of Holyrood house; whither also came secretly the Earls of Huntly, Angus, and Erroll. The next day, the King riding at Lauder to visit Chancellor Maitland (who was then sick) these three earls came to His Majesty on the highway; and there humbling themselves, in few words demanded licence to be tried, which His Majesty granted. But the King thereafter, in respect that he had promised both to the Ambassador of England, and to the ministers at Edinburgh, that he should neither receive them, nor admit them to his presence and favour, till they were tried; he directed the master of Glammis and the lord Lindores unto the Ambassador and the ministers, to certify them of their coming to His Majesty on the highway, at such time and place as he looked not for; and, although he had used but some few words unto them, yet he would proceed no further, nor show them any other favour, but according to justice and reason. Then the ministry assembled themselves, by their commissioners at Edinburgh, together with certain barons and bailies of burghs, (the King being then at Jedburgh for some affairs of the commonwealth.) They concluded, all in one voice, some articles to be presently demanded of His Majesty; which I omit to relate, as fitting to be supprest.

Whereupon the affairs of the King and of the Church were directly opposite and repugnant to another, the King caused proclamations to be made, commanding all his lieges and subjects to reset and receive the Earls of Angus, Huntly, and Erroll, which should not be imputed unto them as a crime at any time thereafter; whereby also licence was granted unto them to pass and repass freely in any parts of the country publicly, as best should please them. The ministers, upon the contrary, offered their proclamation in the churches to their parishioners, commanding the people to abhor them, and to refuse their companies in any kind of way, and exhorting all men to be upon their defence, and to arm themselves for expelling of these Earls and their adherents; moreover, the ministry by their solicitations had drawn a great number of people into

Edinburgh. Whereupon His Majesty did call a convention of the estates, and caused a proclamation to be made, and published in divers capital towns of the realm, charging all and sundry His Majesty's subjects, of what estate, quality, or degree soever, that none of them should resort or repair to the burgh of Edinburgh, or place of His Majesty's residence, upon whatsoever colour or pretence, during the handling and ordering of these matters in question, except such persons as were appointed and specially written for, or that did crave and obtain His Majesty's licence for their coming. In this commission, which was appointed at Edinburgh for decision of all controversies, there were nominated six earls, six lords, six barons, six burgesses, and six ministers, elected and chosen by His Majesty and his Council; and although the six ministers were well-qualified men, and such as the rest of the brethren could justly find no fault withal, yet, because they were not nominated by themselves in general voices, they were afraid to be prejudged in their authority and estate; and, therefore, not only opposed against them, but also subnamed them which were chosen by the King and the Council: therefore the King, with advice of his Council, commanded their names to be blotted out, that no minister thereafter should be nominated in commission, but that they all, or some certain number, by command of the rest, should only be supplicants, if they had anything to crave, and no otherwise; and thus were the ministers themselves the cause that their authority was diminished.

The Commissioners did assemble at Edinburgh, as was appointed, and after some few days' disputation and reasoning, amongst divers other things, they decerned that the three Popish Earls and Achindoun should not from henceforth be accused for the crime they were summoned for, founded upon the blanks; but the same to remain abolished and in oblivion, and to be null thereafter; which was proclaimed by edict, at the Market Cross of Edinburgh.

The advertisement of this edict being sent from Edinburgh to the Queen of England by her Ambassador, she sent the Lord South into Scotland, willing the King to remit his lenity towards the Catholic lords, and deal plainly with rigorous justice, as the cause and good reason required. The two Ambassadors of England followed the King from Edinburgh to Stirling, by whose diligence and procurement letters were directed, charging the Roman Catholic Earls to enter their persons in prison, under the pain of treason. There was also a Parliament proclaimed, to be holden the 15th of April next ensuing. In the meantime, great instance was made by the ministers of Scotland and by the Ambassadors of England, that the Roman Catholic lords should be summoned to hear and see the process of forfaulture led against them. In end they do prevail; and direction was given for the same against the Parliament, which was appointed to be in April, 1594. Nevertheless, the Ambassadors of England, and the ministers of Scotland, thinking that the King and his counsellors were more negligent in prosecuting of the Popish lords than was promised or expected; it was secretly devised that the Earl of Bothwell, being an outlaw, should invade Scotland, by the assistance of England, upon two pretences: the first was, that, by the help of the ministers, he might banish the

Popish lords out of the realm of Scotland, and that the Queen of England should support him with money; which, being known and revealed, did so incense the King against her Ambassador, that a special gentleman of the Lord South's was committed to prison in the Castle of Edinburgh, who confessed that, by the command of the Ambassador, he had spoken with the Earl of Bothwell and with Mr. John Colvill (Bothwell's chief counsellor). The second pretence was to revenge the Earl of Murray's death against Huntly and his partakers ; and to fortify his purpose, the Earls of Argyle and Athole should be ready in arms, attending Bothwell's coming, to join with him against Huntly.

The King, hearing of these two pretences, thought it expedient, with advice of his council, to make a general proclamation that no manner of persons should convocate his lieges in arms, for whatsoever occasion, without His Majesty's licence, under the pain of death. Whereupon Bothwell came to Kelso, and from thence to Leith, the 2nd of April, 1594. The King being advertised of his coming, went to sermon that morning in the High Church of Edinburgh, and there, sermon being ended, he made great instance to the people, that they would assist him to suppress their common enemy Bothwell, and to animate the Ministry and the people, he promised, in their presence, that he should never lay down arms, till he either suppressed or banished the Popish lords and their adherents; so the King led the people out of Edinburgh towards Leith; and, betwixt Leith and Edinburgh, there was a company selected out of the army, which, under the conduct of the lord Hume and Wemyss Colvill, should invade Bothwell; who, perceiving the King marching out of Edinburgh, with his army, towards Leith; and seeing that the Earls of Argyle and Athole had failed him, he retires from Leith, with his company, and takes the way to Musselburgh, and so return into England; but the Lord Hume, with his train, overtakes Bothwell beside Duddistone, where, after a little skirmish, the lord Hume was overthrown, and all his people beaten and chased back again to Edinburgh. Bothwell, perceiving that the King was sending more forces against him, retires towards the south borders, and so into England.

The Earl of Bothwell being thus gone, the King returns to Edinburgh, and seeing no other means to satisfy the ministers, and all utterly to suppress Bothwell's rebellion, he condescended to the forfaulture of the Popish lords, being forced to yield to present necessity. A Parliament was holden at Edinburgh the penult day of May, 1594; all and whatsoever petitions then craved by the ministers were assented to by this Parliament, where there were present but only three earls and six lords; by reason whereof things were violently carried by the ministers. The criminal cause of the Popish lords being read and considered by the few number of nobles there present, they would gladly have delayed the determination thereof until a fuller convention of the nobility were assembled; but the ministers and commissioners of burghs, being the greater number, prevailed; and found the hand-writs by witnesses cognosced; the rest was passed over, as proven by presumption; the nobles suspended their voices, because the Popish lords' intentions were not proven judicially; always they were forfaulted and made proscript by plurality of such voices as were there present, and their arms were riven in the justice place, in presence of the Parliament.

These noblemen, being thus forfaulted, the King was also moved to make the Earl of Argyle, his Majesty's lieutenant-general in the north of Scotland, to invade the Earls of Huntly and Erroll; whereupon followed the battle of Glenlivat in October, 1594; which happened as I have declared already; and were afterwards restored the year of God, 1597.

FINIS.

www.ingramcontent.com/pod-product-compliance
Lightning Source LLC
Chambersburg PA
CBHW021143230426
43667CB00005B/228